Reflective Practice

Previous books from this author

SLLA Crash Course: Approaches for Success

Improving Instructional Practice: Resolving Issues in Leadership through Case Studies

Elementary School Principals in Action: Resolving Case Studies in Leadership

Reflective Practice

Case Studies for High School Principals

Wafa Hozien

ROWMAN & LITTLEFIELD
Lanham • Boulder • New York • London

Published by Rowman & Littlefield
A wholly owned subsidiary of The Rowman & Littlefield Publishing Group, Inc.
4501 Forbes Boulevard, Suite 200, Lanham, Maryland 20706
www.rowman.com

Unit A, Whitacre Mews, 26–34 Stannary Street, London SE11 4AB

British Library Cataloguing in Publication Information Available

Library of Congress Cataloging-in-Publication Data

Names: Hozien, Wafa, author.
Title: Reflective practice : case studies for high school principals / Wafa Hozien.
Description: Lanham : Rowman & Littlefield, 2017 |
   Includes bibliographical references.
Identifiers: LCCN 2017059611 (print) | LCCN 2017060092 (ebook)
   ISBN 9781475838572 (electronic) | ISBN 9781475838558 (cloth : alk. paper)
   ISBN 9781475838565 (pbk. : alk. paper)
Subjects: LCSH: High schools—Administration—Case studies. |
   High school principals—Professional relationships—Case studies.
Classification: LCC LB2822 (ebook) |
   LCC LB2822 .H67 2017 (print) DDC 373.12—dc23
LC record available at https://lccn.loc.gov/2017059611

♾™ The paper used in this publication meets the minimum requirements of American National Standard for Information Sciences—Permanence of Paper for Printed Library Materials, ANSI/NISO Z39.48–1992.

Printed in the United States of America

For all those people who have taken the time to guide me
and have supported me in my life, I thank you
and dedicate this book to you.

For those educators who have decided to make
a difference in the lives of future generations,
this book is for you.

Contents

Foreword

FOSTERING SCHOOL ADMINISTRATIVE
DECISION-MAKING PROCESSES

Effective leadership has the ability to serve as a change agent that brings forth the commitment and fortitude to bring about change within the educational sector. Marzano (2003) asserted that leadership is one of the highest significant facets of any transformation or reform movement related to schools. Leaders' decisions and factors that guide their decisions have a colossal impingement on the success of schools and student achievement.

This book offers a unique opportunity to engage in real-life dilemmas, meaningful discussion, lively debate, and serious problem solving with case study material that is both timely and representative of real-life principal interactions and at the same time aligned to latest PSEL (2015) standards so as to further understand the connection to leadership expectations.

The method used in this book seeks to bridge the gap between theory and practice. The cases presented here are written from actual happenings in the news and within schools. Courses and seminars in educational leadership are often criticized as being too theoretical to have any direct relationship to the problems of administrating schools. Here in the following pages, theory meets practice. The PSEL (2015) standards are aligned to each case study so as to give each scenario grounding in the proper leadership context. Using a decision-making approach supports administrators engaging in reflection and seeking understanding so as to resolve the conflict in values proposed by competing arguments. Dr. Hozien lays out the foundation for this by asking what are the issues related to case, what options does the school leader have, and what are the potential consequences to the proposed action, thereby engaging readers in active discussion of the entire composition of the dilemma.

One important function of the job of school is that of school leader concerned with improved staff performance, curriculum development, school climate, and progress in student learning. Another important function is that of manager concerned with scheduling lunchroom, playground, and bus operations, maintaining the physical plant, managing public relations, ordering supplies, and directing nonteaching personnel, to name a few. Both functions comprise time-consuming tasks. The principal is faced with so many hours of time in which to accomplish his duties. It is often difficult to cover everything that must be done satisfactorily and a choice must be made among the many needs of the school. This is what this book is about the decision-making practices of school principals and how to steadily improve these practices through constant open conversations. This book is the door to those constructive conversations for any person seeking to be a school administrator at any level.

In the current day of educational reflection and reform, it behooves the educational establishment, and our society as a whole, to be clear on the aims and direction chosen, as we move toward the process of more effective educational enhancement and attainment. As the world moves through the coming decade and beyond, education will continue to define the ever-evolving American way of life. It will also no doubt set the tone to the extent to which the rest of the world cultivates and educates its citizenry. The continued deliverance of impactful educational strategies and solutions as they relate to issues affecting today's educational direction is of utmost importance.

The urgency of such educational attainment is critical to both the short- and long-term success of the nation's educational process and its overall growth as a nation. As educators venture through the current and coming era of school effectiveness, competence and clearly defined instructional delivery and conceptual leadership tools as suggested by Dr. Hozien's writing will aid in the aim and dialogue for such attainment. In this much-needed assessment and suggestive epilogue of instructive direction, Dr. Hozien has her finger on the pulse of and her eyes clearly focused on what it takes to envision and secure effective school administrative leadership. Because overall enhancement in the area of education is of pinnacle importance and extremely critical to the future of the nation, proficient school principal performance on the part of qualified educators is enormously important. Often educators are left to perform without the aid of "how to" guide(s), road maps or "cookie cutter" solutions, that some believe might aid in finding seemingly perfect solutions for an area of occupation that has no one right or direction to success. In her critical educational exposé, Dr. Hozien is very much on target in her defining dialogue and assessment of directions to take and dialogues to have in route to true educational efficacy.

Given the necessity for effectiveness in this field, tools and information suggested in Dr. Hozien's writings will be exchanged throughout this era of the now perpetual "school improvement process." It is clear that the daily, weekly, monthly, and yearly process of fielding duties, issues, problems, and sometimes roadblocks that are faced in education must be dealt with effectively by school leaders who are clear on what direction to take. The task of identifying, stating, and clarifying the direction to school leadership proficiency will continue to be the focus and the goal of the educational establishments. Dr. Hozien recognizes this and does an excellent job of identifying and highlighting the direction for our school leaders' future in her book.

This book is a valuable resource for university professors, professional development offices, school districts, and seminar leaders. It calls for those who are about to embark on the voyage of school leadership to engage with real-life scenarios and dialogue about them, meaning that the journey begins here for school leaders everywhere with the cases presented here in this text. It is to strengthen the problem-solving experience that the school leader will be faced with daily and routinely. This book prepares school leaders to take on the charge of improving schools for students and the realistic balance that is to foster understanding of the many challenges that the future school leader will face.

Marzano, R. (2003). *What Works in Schools: Translating Research into Action.* Alexandria, VA: Association for Supervision and Curriculum Development.

Randolph Mitchell, PhD
Retired School Principal, Virginia

Introduction

So what is being a principal really about? This is the opportunity to actually practice school leadership skills. Put those skills learned in numerous classes to the test. A principal has to have the humility to learn from all those that are in that school setting. To listen and search for those resources to ensure success for every single student in that building. To be resilient to keep going, to commit to keep improving, to be refined as a school principal.

Years later as a school leader, you should know that you can be a better leader. By listening and understanding how you or others resolve the case studies in this book. Not afraid to make mistakes and understand your weaknesses. So that way you do not have to experience failure again or make the wrong decision again. By understanding your school community and the context of your environment, you can resolve each case study. Open to others' ideas and listen for the opportunity to collaborate to work together in a genuine way to improve student achievement and to make that year the best school year ever.

What we know is that school principals are better together than they are on their own. The school community needs each other to build each other, to celebrate when it is great. In order to cast the vision—where are all of the stakeholders going—the principal needs to ensure that this is the best year ever. But where is the principal taking these students? Staff? This week, next month, next school year—all of those people that as a leader you represent. They need the principal to have a plan to help them execute it. This book helps the school leader understand those nuances and how to make critical decisions so as to have that vision of excellence in their school. That way if the principal comes across any of the case studies presented in this book, one can understand how to resolve them before they emerge. Being proactive is job number one. How to anticipate the actions of others so as to safeguard learning for every student? The principal can then focus on that vision of excellence for every student.

This book is about understanding that being a school principal is an ongoing job that does not stop when the school day is done because the school is constantly in the thoughts of the principal. It has to be because, as the leader, the principal is responsible for faculty, staff, and, most importantly, the students. Sometimes the principal is awake at night thinking through a difficult problem; other times something prevents the school leader from sleeping well or enters a myriad of dreams.

In many ways, school principals are always "on the job" even when they are off or away on vacation, but to maintain one's sanity and a healthy family life, one should make every effort to draw a line in the sand, delineate work from home, and make time for family, especially doing things to let one's own family know that they are just as important as those children at school.

Some of the case studies in this book are based on real-life news events. The references at the end of the book are a part of the inspiration for the case studies that take place in this book.

ORGANIZATION OF THIS BOOK

This educational leadership case study book consists of five sections found in this book and two sections found online.

Title and PSEL (2015) Standard Alignment
Background
Issue
Dilemma
Questions for Discussion

ONLINE WEBSITE

Resolutions
Abridged Case Study Version

What is different about this book?

For those educators teaching online and preparing future school principals or superintendents, there are abridged versions of each case study provided for this text online, under "Additional Resources" and then "Online Version" on the Rowman and Littlefield website for this book. That means that when teaching online, the material is provided and can be included in a brief PowerPoint presentation, while the students prior to class can read the full-length case study in this book. Furthermore, the possible solutions were left out of this text so as to include more case studies. The possible resolutions to the case studies and the online format for the case studies can be found online on the Rowman and Littlefield website for this book: *Reflective Practice: Case Studies for High School Principals*: https://rowman.com/.

This book is aligned to the Professional Standards for Educational Leaders, or PSEL, rewritten in 2015, that were designed to influence the preparation of principals, guide states in the development of their own state-wide principal standards, and serve as a tool for licensure or evaluation. The descriptors accompanying the standards have been omitted here for the sake of brevity (Hozien, 2017). The ten standards address a principal's need to promote the success of all students (NPBEA, 2015); briefly, they are provided for you here.

Standard 1. Mission, Vision, and Core Values
Standard 2. Ethics and Professional Norms
Standard 3. Equity and Cultural Responsiveness
Standard 4. Curriculum, Instruction, and Assessment
Standard 5. Community of Care and Support for Students
Standard 6. Professional Capacity of School Personnel
Standard 7. Professional Community for Teachers and Staff
Standard 8. Meaningful Engagement of Families and Community
Standard 9. Operations and Management
Standard 10. School Improvement

Chapter 1

The Mission and Vision
of Schooling

CASE STUDY: *CASTING THE WRONG VOTE*
SUBURBAN MIDDLE SCHOOL GRADES 6–8
MISSION, VISION, AND CORE VALUES, 1G
COMMUNITY OF CARE AND SUPPORT FOR STUDENTS, 5A

Background

The most recent presidential election in the United States was one full of anxiety and emotion for a lot of voters, and this stress carried over into the workplace and in the schools. Students for their teachers argued about presidential choices, and often the students joined in the arguments in the classroom.

Students and teachers were quick to take sides, arguing in favor of or against a particular candidate. Often the discussions would quickly become heated as tempers flared and the emotions boiled over.

Principal Dana Adams was concerned about the interruption these behaviors were causing. When she met with her teachers about their pacing with their curriculum guides, some of the teachers mention that they have fallen behind because they had taken the time to discuss and debate politics in the classroom instead. It was easy to get off track, they said.

Mrs. Adams asked all of the teachers to refrain from discussing politics in the classroom. Furthermore, she asked the teachers what support they needed from her. The teachers asked the principal to make a public statement that the campus would be a politics-free zone, where students, faculty, and staff would avoid discussing politics.

The principal said she could do that for her teachers. Later that day, she posted a statement on the school's social media page, stating that beginning immediately South Middle School was the politics-free zone. "Every

1

American citizen has the right his or her own opinion," she wrote, "but the discussion of these opinions cannot take place during instructional time at our school because they prevent children from learning the curriculum and preparing for their high-stakes assessment of the end-of-the-year. Therefore, I respectfully asked that all political conversations be limited to the home and other non-instructional environments."

Leonard Gibbons was an eighth grade student at South Middle School in the suburbs of a large metropolitan area. Without realizing what's the post on the school social media page said, Leonard's mom let her son wear his Make America Great Again cap to school.

Upon entering his classroom, several of the students guffawed, saying, "You voted for him? Happy to be so stupid? What's wrong with you anyway?"

As Leonard was trying to formulate an answer, his teacher stepped in and asked them to remove the hat. Taking Leonard aside, the teacher explained in a quiet voice that the school classroom was to be a politics-free zone. There would be no more political discussion about the candidates or the election. As a result, the best course of action would be to leave the hat with the teacher for safekeeping. Leonard could come by and pick up the hat at the end of the day.

"What about her?" Leonard asked. He pointed to one of his classmates who was wearing an "I'm with her" T-shirt. "How come she still gets to wear that shirt?"

The teacher explained that T-shirt was not nearly as offensive as the cap that said Make America Great Again. "It doesn't upset people the way your hat does," said the teacher.

Rather than argue with his teacher, Leonard remain silent, deciding that the best course of action would be to pick up his hat at the end of the day.

When the bell rang to dismiss school, Leonard went by his teacher's classroom to pick up his hat. The teacher handed it to him.

"I have to apologize—the hat was in my desk drawer, and I'm afraid that I spilled a little of my soda at lunch, and some of it got on the hat. But other than that, your hat is as good as new," said the teacher.

Leonard looked at the stain that the spill had left behind. Again he didn't say anything. He took his hat and ran off to find his bus.

On the bus, Leonard decided he would wear his hat, proudly displaying his choice of presidential candidate.

No sooner he put the hat on his head than several of the students began heckling him. They called Leonard a racist, a bigot, and a Nazi for his support to Trump. Although Leonard tried to explain that he was none of those things, one of the boys shoved him, throwing Leonard off balance and causing him to hit the metal edge of the seat in front of him.

When Leonard sat back up, he was missing part of a tooth and his mouth was bleeding. He began to cry.

"What's the matter, poor baby, did you fall and go boom-boom? Serves you right, you little Trumpster!" said the students around Leonard. What they did not realize was that Leonard had videotaped the entire incident by activating the video camera and sound on his phone.

When his bus stop arrived, Leonard made his way to the exit and walked the rest of the way home.

Leonard's mom panicked the moment she saw him. "What happened to you," she asked. "Do you know who did this?"

Leonard held out his phone.

Mrs. Gibbons made two very quick phone calls, one to the dentist to see if she could get her son an emergency appointment before the dentist office closed. The second phone call was to the local news station, who agreed to send a reporter to meet Mrs. Gibbons and Leonard at the dentist's office.

That evening, the news station reported that a middle school student had been wrongfully beaten on the school bus because of his support for a particular presidential candidate. They had called the school talk to the principal, and Mrs. Adams had told them that she had just declared the school to be a politics-free zone. No students were supposed to discuss politics in the school environment, including on buses. Leonard was in the wrong because he wore the hat that said Make America Great Again. She also said that she would follow up regarding the behavior of the other students on the bus.

Mrs. Gibbons was the first person waiting to speak to the principal the next morning.

Issue

Principal Dana Adams supported her teachers' request to declare the school a politics-free zone so that they can focus on instruction. Mrs. Adams posted her request on the school's social media page.

Dilemma

Even though the request to create a politics-free zone in school had been made on social media, not everyone was aware of the request. The students wore campaign clothing to school the very next day. One student wore a "I'm with her" T-shirt and was told nothing about the clothing she was wearing. Another student, Leonard Gibbons, was wearing a Make America Great Again hat.

His teacher requested that Leonard take off the hat and leave it with the teacher for safekeeping. When Leonard picked up his hat at the end of this school day, the hat was stained with soda that the teacher had accidentally spilled on it. Leonard took his hat and wore it home on the school bus, where he was bullied and beaten.

Leonard's mother called the news media to spread the story of what had happened to her son, and she shared his video of the incident with the news station, who blurred the faces of the other students.

When she learned of the social media page request, she was furious that the principal had called children's homes "non-instructional environments." She is in the principal's office, demanding to see the principal and wanting to know what will be done about her child.

Questions for Discussion

1. Can a school declare a politics-free zone? Why would it be in the students' best interests to do so?
2. In what ways could be excluding politics at school a bad idea?
3. Do you think that the students on the bus deserve any consequences for their actions? If so what do you recommend?
4. How likely is it that Leonard wore the hat to antagonize students because he had been videotaping his ride home on the bus? What consequences, if any, should Leonard face?
5. What fault, if any, lies with the teacher? Was the teacher being unfair? How so?
6. What would have been a better way to inform the parents than sending a request through social media?

CASE STUDY: *88 TIMES*
URBAN HIGH SCHOOL GRADES 9–12
MISSION, VISION, AND CORE VALUES, 1C
EQUITY AND CULTURAL RESPONSIVENESS, 3A, B

Background

Ted Robbins is the principal at Franklin High School. The inner city school building is a multistory building with red brick and masonry cornices. The building is a wonderful example of construction from another century. There are a high ceilings and antique wooden floors, and, not surprisingly, there are plenty of rooms to host everything from small meetings in several of the conference rooms or two larger group gatherings in the cafeteria or the auditorium.

For this reason and more, many groups outside the school like to rent space in the building after school hours for meetings. Principal Robbins discovered that he could rent out unused space after school hours. He charged groups that wanted to meet at the school a nominal fee plus the cost of the security guard and custodial cleanup afterward.

The principal quickly discovered that even nominal fees added up after a while, and he was able to set aside money that the rented spaces earned throughout the year. At the end of the year, he used the money for incentives and rewards for his students. Thanks to this little enterprise, the school was able to provide some nice awards for the students. They gave away everything from bicycles to tablets and even smartphones. Sometimes the awards consisted of gift cards to local retailers.

Mr. Robbins knew most of the groups that met after school in his building. Each year at the beginning of the year he would work with various club presidents and plan a schedule for when they wanted to hold their meetings. Most of the meetings took place Monday through Thursday evenings. The various spaces in the building were occupied by the Boy Scouts of America, the Girl Scouts, a local affiliation of business professionals, and occasionally a speaking group rented out one of the larger areas old in which to have training sessions and contests.

This year three new groups also wanted to rent space in the building. The first group was the Antioch Baptist church, who wanted to meet on Sunday mornings. The second group was a group called Horns and Blood, and they were a group of occultists who wanted to rent space on Friday nights. The final group was called the 88s, and they were led by a couple of men in the community who advertised the club as a group of Geocachers who would also include some of the high school students in their membership.

Principal Robbins looked over the application and pulled out his set of stamps. On two of the applications, he immediately stamped DENIED. The third one is stamped approved, and he called the leaders of the Geocachers to let them know that they had been able to secure their space for the entire year.

The 88s often forgot to take their banner with them after the meeting. Sometimes the custodian who retrieved the banner left it in the administration office so that one of the club members could pick it during the week. On several occasions, the custodian forgot all about the banner and left it in the classroom.

Principal Robbins began to notice recruiting posters around the campus. The Boy Scouts put up a few posters, and so did the Girl Scouts, but the 88s seemed to go all out for their recruiting efforts. They seemed to have posters everywhere. Some of the posters said join the 88s, and others said 884R. On a few of the posters were the letters FHS4R. The principal didn't think about it too much, and he went on his way.

During the weekend, Robins flipped on the news, and he did a double take. There on the screen, being restrained by two police officers, was one of his math teachers. She was screaming obscenities at another group of people, calling them racists, bigots, and skinheads. Robbins looked away from her and at the group. He recognized several people from the 88s, and standing with them were more than a few Franklin High School students. They were protesting as neo-Nazis. They also mentioned that they met regularly at the high school. One of the banners they had with them said, "follow us at #FHSR4."

"We won't stop until we have 88 sites at schools around the nation. First Saratoga Springs High School in Florida, and now Franklin High School, too! We are coming to You next!" said the club president.

On Monday morning, the superintendent of schools was waiting for Mr. Robbins when he arrived at work.

"Have you seen what's been going on in the news and on social media?" she asked. Mr. Robbins said that he had seen the news but was not aware of anything on social media.

"Are they talking about Ms. Buford, the math teacher?" he asked.

"Not as much as the discussion about the neo-Nazi club you allowed on this campus. How could you?" asked the superintendent.

"They told me they were Geocachers. I believed them," said Mr. Robbins. "What was I supposed to do?"

The superintendent explained that the club had been on campus to recruit new members. Apparently they had been effective at it because more than 100 Franklin high school students boasted about being members of the 88s. She explained that the eighth letter of the alphabet is H and 8-8 stood for H-H, or Heil Hitler.

"But that's not the half of it," she continued. "The FHS4R that you have been seeing on posters and banners everywhere stands for Franklin High School, Fourth Reich. This group has several social media accounts, and students at your campus are following them and participating in them by posting discriminatory statements."

Mr. Robbins was dumbfounded.

"You will come up with a plan of action to eliminate this group from the campus, and I want that plan in my office before 5 o'clock today."

With that, superintendent walked out of Mr. Robbin's office.

The secretary walked into his office next, with a large stack of memos.

"These are the phone calls that have come in so far," she said. "Most are from parents, but there are some from news stations and even the ACLU. They are all waiting to hear from you."

Issue

Principal Robbins has a hate group that meets regularly at his campus. Not only had they been meeting at the school but they also had been actively recruiting students as members. The hate group had been allowed to advertise freely on the campus for student members.

One of the high school teachers went to a rally over the weekend and was detained by police when she began yelling slurs at the hate group. They, in turn, were not yelling at her, but they did announce that they had a goal of being in the eighty-eight different high schools around the nation. Franklin was just one of them.

Mr. Robbins learned from the superintendent that more than 100 of his students had joined the 88s, and even more than that they are following them on social media platforms.

Dilemma

The superintendent of schools met Mr. Robbins at his office on Monday immediately following the news cast.

She explained to him exactly who the 88s are. Now Mr. Robbins faces the hate group that is also known to be violent, and he has allowed them access to the school building. The 88s have recruited many of the high school students, and even more are following them in social media.

The superintendent wants the 88s removed from the campus, and she also wants the principal to protect the students who are connected to the 88s, through either membership or social media.

The news media, parents, and even the ACLU also are trying to get in touch with the principal.

Mr. Robbins has time until 5 p.m. to come up with a solution.

Questions for Discussion

1. Is there anything wrong with getting students expensive gifts as an incentive? Explain the challenges.
2. Why would the principal not approve the applications for the Antioch Baptist Church and for the group known as Blood and Horns?
3. What should the principal have done about the 88s?
4. What action should Principal Robbins take in regard to the teacher who was yelling slurs at the process on Saturday. Why?
5. What course of action do you recommend that Mr. Robbins take so that he can resolve his dilemma by 5 p.m.? How can he get a resolution that quickly?

CASE STUDY: *DO AS I SAY*
RURAL HIGH SCHOOL GRADES 9–12
MISSION, VISION, AND CORE VALUES 1B, D

Background

Jo Luna was the principal at Creek High School, Home of the Fighting Warriors. She'd been principal at this campus for five years, and during that time, the football team had gone to state twice and won the championship title. The campus was also a nationally recognized school.

The Warriors were known far and wide. The high school had a strong reputation for athletics and academics, and the surrounding schools recognized that the students and their teachers took competition as seriously as a group of warriors on the battlefield. When other schools saw the iconic mascot of an Indian chief in full headdress, they knew they'd have a fight on their hands for the trophy or designation of first place.

The Indian chief mascot had been selected years and years ago. Since then, the school developed many traditions around the theme of the Creek Indians. The campus had the Arrow Club (devoted to developing goals and staying on target), Wigwam Weekend (the annual school dance and sleepover in the gym), and the Sweat Lodge (the weight room for the athletes).

The school motto at Creek High School was Honor and Dignity in Everything, and it was something that the principal and the faculty took very seriously. Anytime a child was disciplined, it was done with love and respect for the child. Mrs. Luna made sure that the teenager was always honored and could retain his or her dignity, regardless of what had happened. That meant not singling out students during class for something they did wrong. That meant not belittling students, and it also meant listening to what the kids had to say.

The campus climate was one of love and respect, although occasionally there were tiffs and spats.

The community loved Creek High School, and they loved the principal who ran the campus. As traumatic as high school could be, the parents at least knew that their children were in the best environment possible. They were proud that their children were part of the fighting Warriors. Many of the parents themselves had gone to Creek High School, and the legacy of having one's kids go to the same school was a community tradition.

Principal Luna was shocked when she opened the letter from the American Civil Liberty Union (ACLU). The ACLU wanted Creek High School to change its name and to change its Indian mascot to something less defamatory. In addition, any school activities that referred to Indian traditions were not allowed. The campus would have to rename all of its clubs and activities, because any reference to Native Americans was considered derogatory and racist.

The principal called for a meeting with the campus advisory committee. She showed them the letter that she had received from the ACLU.

"What do you think?" the principal asked.

"Wow," said Mr. Lightfoot, the math department head. "The ACLU seems pretty serious about this. It looks like everything has to go. They didn't even give us a very long the window of time to make all of the necessary changes. Look, it says we have 90 days to make all of the changes."

"I know," said the principal. "I don't see how it's even possible to do what they're asking within that timeframe."

"Maybe they just did that scare us," said one of the other teachers on the council. "To me, it sounds like they are bullying us into political correctness. Is that even what we want?"

Another teacher said, "How did the ACLU even know about our school? Do they just go around looking for things to change?"

Principal Luna asked everyone in the room what he or she wanted as the outcome of this requested change. Words the teachers in agreement that the names should change, or should Creek High School remain the home of the fighting Warriors?

"You know," said Mrs. Luna, "I really think we ought to keep the name. We have been Creek High School for as long as anyone can remember. The school building was named after the tribe that lived in this area. The Creek were noble warriors. They were powerful and wise. They revered tradition and honored their communities."

"Oh that's ridiculous," said Mr. Franklin. "The Creek were some of the first Indians to adopt the ways of the Europeans who were pushing them off their lands. They wore clothing from England, and they even owned slaves. Many of them converted to Christianity. So much for that whole dignity and honor garbage. I say the name changes, and the sooner, the better."

The committee talked about the issue some more and decided it would be a good idea to get the parents and community involved in making the decision about whether to change the name or keep the name.

One week later, Principal Luna took the issue to the community. Again she shared the contents of the letter from the ACLU, and again a lengthy discussion ensued.

Some parents and community members argued that the name did indeed have to be changed. To use the mascot of an Indian chief was demeaning and racist. These were different times than those of the past, and society had become more respectful than it had been in the past.

Mr. Franklin was present at the meeting, and he agreed wholeheartedly. "Let's have a vote NOW!" he demanded.

"Not so fast," said one of the parents. Mr. Weatherford was the oldest man in town, and if you wanted to know about history, you went to him. "This high school was named after the Creek Indians because they represented the five civilized tribes. That's not too different from today, where all races can come together and respect each other—with honor and dignity." He winked at Principal Luna before continuing. "We are the fighting Warriors, not the fighting redskins or indigenous persons. And just so that all of you know, the image you use for the mascot is that of the Creek Chief Red Eagle. You may know him as William Weatherford. He was my great-great-great-great-great-great grandfather, and it was the fighting he saw at the Ft. Mimms massacre that turned him into an honorable and dignified man. Although he was a warrior, he also loved peace. I say we keep the name."

The principal decided to take a vote by silent ballot at the meeting. The teachers distributed slips of colored paper to everyone in the room.

"Okay, everyone, take a short break and we'll tell you the outcome in just a bit," said Mrs. Luna.

She was hoping to reach an outcome with honor and dignity.

Issue

Creek High School is named after a prominent tribe of Native Americans. The school mascot is an Indian chief, and the students call themselves the fighting warriors. Many of the club's cultural activities center around similar activities of the locally indigenous persons.

The teachers and the community can see good reasons for making the changes, but they can also see why making any changes would be bad. The parents are also split evenly on the issue.

Should the school keep the name or change it?

Dilemma

The school principal has received a letter from the ACLU demanding that the school cease dishonoring Native Americans by using their tribe name and a picture of an Indian chief as their mascot. They have a very short time frame in which to make the change.

The teachers were evenly split on whether to change everything or whether they should fight back. It's likely that one of the high school teachers is responsible for contacting the ACLU to get the school name and mascot changed to something more politically appropriate.

A vote will decide whether to take the ACLU's advice and change the name or whether it would be in the best interest of the town to fight the request to change.

Mrs. Luna wants to keep the name, so does the town's oldest resident, Mr. Weatherford. When she counts the votes and announces which direction the campus will take for its future, should she tell the truth or select the option she favors the most, and tell everyone that that was the winning and final decision?

Questions for Discussion

1. Can the ACLU make these demands? Do they have any power over the school?
2. Explain why using the names, images, or defamatory slurs surrounding Native Americans is inappropriate.
3. What is the right choice to make in this situation? Explain why.

4. How would your decision be different if you knew that 65 percent of the student population and the community were Native Americans who were descendants of the Creek Indians?
5. Should the principal tell the truth about the final vote or swing it her way? Why?

Chapter 2

Promoting Ethics through Example

CASE STUDY: *EXTRAMARITAL EXTRA CREDIT*
SUBURBAN HIGH SCHOOL GRADES 9–12
ETHICS AND PROFESSIONAL NORMS, 2A, F

Background

Sharon Holman just graduated from college two years ago. She was young, beautiful and her students adored her.

Ryan Vickers, the principal at Blue Ridge High School, had hesitated in hiring her because Ms. Holman was so close in age to the students that she would be teaching. The young candidate had stellar references, a solid education in teaching, and she was full of enthusiasm for working with teens. Everyone Principal Vickers spoke to said Ms. Holman was mature and could be trusted to have good judgment.

Ms. Holman taught junior-level English. She was exceptionally gifted in teaching writing, and in the past two years, nearly 95 percent of her students met or exceeded the writing standards for the SAT. The principal thought Ms. Holman was a dream come true because his school was now a top performer in the state. Even better, more of the Blue Ridge High School students were getting accepted at colleges. He was certain this was because of Ms. Holman's writing instruction.

Ms. Holman worked hard and dedicated her time to her students. She told them that because she was single, she had all the time in the world to help them with their homework after school. All they had to do was message or call her and she would make herself available for them.

Sometimes Ms. Holman met students at a local coffee shop to help them with their studies, and sometimes she met them at their houses. The parents were very impressed that a teacher would devote so much time to helping students. She even worked around the students' schedules for athletics and extra-curricular activities and their jobs. What the parents did not know was that Ms. Holman also tutored a select few of her students at her apartment. Most of the time these tutoring sessions occurred in groups three to six students.

One of the students she tutored was Randy Nelson, the quarterback on the football team. Randy was a junior, just turned seventeen, and there had already been talk that Randy could easily turn pro after playing college ball.

One evening, Randy stopped by his teacher's apartment to request help with a project. Ms. Holman agreed.

By the end of the week, the teacher and her student had had carnal knowledge of each other. The behavior of the teacher and her student changed in the classroom. Ms. Holman would look at Randy until she caught his eye. She would wink or pucker her lips ever so slightly, and Randy would grin. Then some of his classmates began teasing him about being the teacher's pet.

The quarterback went to the counselor to ask for a class change. He told the counselor he didn't want to be in that room anymore. The counselor explained that there were no open slots, and that without a really good reason for the request, no change could be made.

Outside of school, Randy and Sharon tried to see each other as often as possible. Randy went to most of Sharon's tutoring sessions just so they could be together. Randy's parents were impressed that he wanted to spend so much time working on his studies. It wasn't long before Randy's teammates figured out what was going on. They wanted to know all of the details about their quarterback's affair with the teacher.

"Look at this," said Randy. "I even have pictures."

The teammates' eyes widened when they saw the pictures. Randy reminded his teammates that they were sworn to secrecy and could not say anything how about his tryst with the English teacher.

Principal Vickers was sitting in the bleachers at one of the campus football games. The Blue Ridge Raiders were winning again, and the crowd loved Ryan. He was a truly gifted athlete. Between the plays, the principal overheard two of the parents talking. They were discussing a relationship between some cougar and her young lover.

A young lover was none another than quarterback Randy Nelson. Principal Vickers was surprised at Randy's prowess. He was even more surprised when he heard the rest of the conversation.

"Supposedly it's one of the teachers," said the first parent.

"There's no way," said the second parent. "Something like that would never be a secret. That kind of news would get spread everywhere."

"That's true," said the first parent. "You watch. I'll bet it's all over social media before we even know it."

Ryan Vickers had overheard the entire conversation, but he couldn't decide whether he should confront the two parents and push for more information, or if he should secretly try to figure it out on his own.

He chose the latter course of action.

Randy Nelson was not the only one who shared pictures from his conquest. Sharon also posted a few of the less outrageous photos on her social media. The photos showed her with a handsome and young-looking boyfriend.

Several of Sharon's friends asked about him, but she would not reveal the name of her boyfriend.

When report cards came out at the end of the six weeks, Randy had made a perfect score in Ms. Holman's class. Several of his friends on the football team were jealous because they did more work than their friend in that class but still received lower grades. The boys complained to counselor about how unfair Ms. Holman's grading practices were.

"Yeah, it's obvious that if you sleep with the teacher," said Ben Griffin, "that you automatically get an A in class."

"Dude, that's supposed to be a secret," said one of the boys.

The counselor asked the boys for clarification.

"Everyone knows Randy Nelson is sleeping with Ms. Holman. They have been at it for about six weeks, and it's unfair," said Ben.

It's more than unfair, thought the counselor to herself. She knew she had to let the principal know immediately.

Issue

A young and attractive high school English teacher has a reputation for helping students achieve outstanding scores on their college entrance exams. In the two years she's been teaching at Blue Ridge High School, the school's students have earned many accolades and been accepted into prestigious colleges.

Many attributed the student success to her willingness to devote additional time to tutoring students, even away from school. This time was not approved by the school, not did the administration know when or where the tutoring took place.

Principal Ryan Vickers has been happy with Ms. Holman's performance until he discovered that she was having an affair with one of her students, a seventeen-year-old football player.

He heard the first rumor of the affair at a football game, where two of the parents were talking about the relationship, but he did not pursue the matter.

Instead, the principal learned about the teacher-student affair from the high school counselor. She learned about it from some of the players on the football team, who had seen pictures of their quarterback with their English teacher.

Dilemma

Principal Vickers allowed off-campus tutoring to occur without approving or stopping it. Obviously, Ms. Holman was tutoring beyond the school day, and she had a reputation for going out of her way to help students outside of the school day. By not addressing the likelihood that it was happening, Mr. Vickers shares a degree of complicity in the situation.

In addition, he failed to speak up at the football game when he overheard the two parents talking about the affair one of his students was having with an older woman—especially when the parents mentioned they heard it might be a teacher.

By the time the counselor came to report the situation, the secret was out, and clues had posted all over social media—on the quarterback's pages and the teacher's pages, and these pages had been liked and shared.

Questions for Discussion

1. What are the first steps the principal needs to take after hearing the news about the affair from the counselor?
2. Should the principal have put a stop to the tutoring going on outside the school day or is there a way to keep the teacher and the students safe from any accusations or indiscretions?
3. Should he have asked the parents for more information at the football game and what is his liability for not doing so?
4. Who from central office needs to be involved in the situation?
5. What recommendations do you have for managing the social media in the situation?
6. Should the principal change Randy's grade to one that reflects his performance in class instead of one that reflects his performance outside class? Why or why not?

CASE STUDY: *DRUG BUST*
RURAL MIDDLE SCHOOL GRADES 6–8
OPERATIONS AND MANAGEMENT, 9
ETHICS AND PROFESSIONAL NORMS, 2A

Background

Lance Green was the school secretary at Deerfield Middle School. He enjoyed his work in this position because, frankly, he was one of few males who worked in the office. It was a great place to meet women—teachers and parents. He also liked working with the middle school students who came by his desk to say hello.

There were several students who visited Lance regularly. They would stop by for just a few minutes before going to their next class, sometimes exchanging pleasantries and sometimes exchanging small items, like a piece of chocolate or other similarly packaged item.

The principal, Betty Conway, thought it was great that the students routinely stopped by the office to say hello, and she didn't think anything else about it.

Lance not only helped the principal but also helped the teachers with getting their grades in at the end of each grading period. He was the one who opened and closed the grading window for posting the grades, and if teachers need an extension, he usually could make it happen. The teachers appreciated it everything that he did for them. They often brought him small treats as a thank-you for everything he did for them. The teachers found that they could confide in him as well.

Susan Armstrong, a new social studies teacher, often went to Lance before having to go to principal. She thought it was far easier to talk to Lance than it was to talk to Principal Conway. It seemed like the principal was always busy and didn't have time for silly questions.

"That's fine," said Lance. "I've been here long enough that I pretty much know how Ms. Conway would answer almost anything you could ask, and if I don't know the answer, I'll make sure that you get in to see her." Ms. Armstrong was happy that she had such a great ally in the office.

That's why when she discovered what some of her students were horsing around with in the classroom, she took it to Lance during her conference period. If it was what she thought it might be, she would likely be severely reprimanded for having such poor behavior management skills. Ms. Armstrong handed the packet of white powder to Lance.

"What do you think this is? Ms. Armstrong asked. "Were they just playing around or is this the real deal? Were they doing drugs in my classroom?"

Lance opened the packet of white powder. He moistened a finger, touched the powder, and then put it in his mouth.

"Well, I guess so," said Lance. "This tastes like the real stuff. How about if I keep this and give it to Ms. Conway. She'll take care of it, and you take care of class," he said.

Ms. Armstrong went back to teach class feeling certain that Lance would take care of everything. She was expecting Ms. Conway to walk into her room at any moment. By the end of the week, however, Ms. Armstrong not heard anything from Ms. Conway. The teacher thought it odd that the principal didn't say anything. Principal Conway did not even address her at the faculty meeting. It was almost as though the principal had no knowledge of what happened.

Another week went by, and Ms. Armstrong decided to ask Ms. Conway about it, but she wanted to do it without anyone else around, especially if she was going to be yelled at.

Lance arrived at school early in the morning, and he was usually one of the first ones to leave at the end of the day, so Ms. Armstrong waited until Lance left. Ms. Conway's door was closed, and she was talking on the phone. She sat outside the principal's office, waiting for her to open the door. When Ms. Conway stepped outside her door, she seemed surprised to see the social studies teacher.

"What are you doing here?" she asked.

"Waiting to talk to you," said Ms. Armstrong.

"Why didn't you make an appointment with Lance? I would've seen you much earlier than now. You would not have had to wait as long," said the principal.

"I think this has to do with Lance, in some part," said Ms. Armstrong. She told him about the white powder she had found in her students' possession in the classroom, and that she had given it to Lance. He had assured her see that he would talk to the principal.

"He never said anything to me," said Ms. Conway, "however, I will see to it that the matter is taken care of."

The next day Ms. Conway asked Lance to step inside her office. She wanted an explanation for why she had not been told students had drugs in their possession.

Lance told her that it had slipped his mind.

Ms. Conway had her suspicions. She asked a few of the seasoned teachers if they had had any unusual dealings with Lance. A couple of them told her they usually had as little to do with him as possible.

"We just turn in grades and that's about it. However, some of the students really like him a lot. They like to hang out around his desk, and he's always giving them little things. They give him stuff, too."

Ms. Conway decided that something didn't sound right and she needed an investigation. She would have to get the district involved.

The investigation confirmed Ms. Conway's suspicions. Lance had been selling drugs from his desk in the front office without any of the other office staff, the teachers, or the principal finding out until now. When questioned, Lance revealed that he had brought some of the drugs to school to sell. Some of the drugs he took from Ms. Conway's desk.

He knew that the principal routinely picked up contraband from students and threw it in the upper right-hand desk drawer of her desk, and then she forgot about it. The drawer was rarely locked, and its contents were cluttered, strewn with small office supplies, a few scattered joints and assorted tablets.

Lance could take something from the drawer, and Ms. Conway would never notice it was missing.

Lance had been selling drugs the principal had confiscated from students and never followed up with.

Issue

A new student with limited English-speaking skills enrolls at Jefferson High School. The other students make fun of her and begin bullying her in the classroom and beyond. Some of the students get Miranda's mobile phone number so that they can harass her electronically. They think no one will find out if they do their bullying through the computer and the mobile phone. Miranda however finds all of the cyberbullying overwhelming, and she does not know how to deal with the messages. Her parents also are unaware of any cyberbullying. They are not familiar with many of the social media platforms used in America and so they do not monitor their daughter's social media activities.

When the principal asked the teachers about cyberbullying, not all of the teachers were even sure what they should look for or what cyberbullying was.

Dilemma

Ms. Conway, the principal, routinely threw contraband and drug paraphernalia in one of her desk drawers. She always intended to follow up with the students and dispose of the drugs, but she always forgot. As a result, her desk always had some illegal substance in it until she would remember to clean out her desk and flush away the substances.

What she did not realize was that her campus secretary Lance had been pilfering drugs from her desk and selling them back to the kids at school. He was selling other drugs to the students, as well, and this had been going on for some time.

Lance was a self-appointed gatekeeper between the teachers and the principal, and he determined who needed to see the principal and who did not.

Questions for Discussion

1. What issues should the principal address with Lance?
2. What should the principal do if Lance cannot produce the packet of white powder that Ms. Armstrong gave him?
3. What's the problem with the contraband in the principal's desk drawer?
4. Should the principal have known that Lance was screening the requests to see her?
5. To whom and does the principal need to report Lance. What follow-up should happen with Ms. Armstrong and the students?

CASE STUDY: *BULLY BRAVADO*
SUBURBAN HIGH SCHOOL GRADES 9–12
ETHICS AND PROFESSIONAL NORMS, 2D
COMMUNITY OF CARE AND SUPPORT FOR STUDENTS, 5D

Background

Principal Mike Miller has been at Kennedy High School for at least two decades. During his leadership, he had seen plenty of changes in education.

Mr. Miller became a principal after ten successful years as a football coach. It was only natural that he move into administration, and high school suited him perfectly. While the principal at Kennedy, Mr. Miller had seen changes in learning standards, community morals, and expectations of what the schools should do for children.

Some of the changes, providing free lunches for the kids, he liked. It meant that students would get a warm meal during the day, and that was important, especially, because it was the only meal some of the students got. The principal knew that oftentimes his students did not eat at all on the weekend. When the school was also able to add breakfast to what they could offer their students, Mr. Miller thought that that was even better.

Other changes that he had seen in education was a steep rise in how many students went home to empty houses because their parents were working.

As a result, Kennedy High School sought to fill the gaps. Rather than send kids home right after school, those students who didn't have jobs could attend tutoring or participate in diverse extracurricular activities. Kennedy offered a variety of clubs so that every student could find his or her niche, and have a group of like-minded friends with whom to hang out.

The teachers sponsored clubs for guitar, chess, music appreciation, running, yoga, writing, programming, careers and trades, reading, fashion, debate, politics, and more. As Principal Miller liked to say, "If you can't find it here at Kennedy, it doesn't exist."

He was a little surprised at a request to offer an LGBTQIA club on the campus, but met with interested students and their sponsors and decided to approve it. The students were ecstatic to form a group of peers with whom they could relate and identify.

The club wanted to participate in many of the other school activities, like the football games and dances.

At homecoming, like so many of the Kennedy High School clubs, the LGBTQIA club wanted to show their team spirit. They spent several weekends preparing beautiful banners for display at the football stadium. These banners consisted of encouraging words for the football team and also had gay pride flags painted on them.

The club arrived at the stadium early to post their banners in various locations. Then they went to dinner at a local fast-food restaurant before the game. When they completed their meal, the club returned to the stadium to take their seats in the stands. They planned to proudly wave their gay pride rainbow flags and support their football team.

As they enter the stadium, they looked about for their banners.

The banners were no longer hanging from the rails. Other banners had been affixed along the rails in place of the gay pride banners. Upon closer look, the club members saw that their banners had been torn apart and either left on the ground in shreds or stuffed in nearby trash cans.

"They can't do that to us," said the club president. "It's not fair. We are here in support of the football team just like anyone else."

The teacher sponsor asked the club to remain together as a group while she went to speak to the coach. When she asked him what happened, he told her, "My team didn't want the support of a bunch of weirdos. There's no room here for gay pride. We have Kennedy pride, and that's all we need." He also called the club members several other derogatory names before the teacher could stop him.

The teacher tried to argue with him again, but the game was about to start and he turned away from her to focus on his job.

When the teacher went back to the stands where the LGBTQIA club was, she noticed that the group was huddled together, trying to look inconspicuous. The teacher asked them what was going on, and several club members told her that the students around them had been calling the club members names and making them feel persecuted. They were too afraid to even go to the restroom or the concession stand by themselves.

The bullies had made the club members feel horrible.

Their teacher stayed with them throughout the game, and at the end, they walked out together as a group to make sure that everyone was safe.

There were still jeers from several students who said things like, "Oh, sure, just wait until you're alone. We'll get you then."

The next day their teacher sponsor met with Principal Miller.

"I can't believe how my students were bullied at the game last night," she said. "And it began with the football coach. He let his football players rip down our banners. We made them in support of that football team, and that's how they treat their fellow students. It's not okay."

"I can understand where they're coming from," said Principal Miller. "I too was once a football coach, and nothing but nothing gets in the way of team spirit."

"We were there to show our spirit," the teacher sponsor responded. "Obviously it wasn't appreciated. What are you going to do when my LGBTQIA students want to go to a school dance together, like Homecoming or the Prom? Because if you don't let them go."

Issue

For the first time in the past thirty years of education, Principal Mark Miller has approved the charter membership of the first LGBTQIA club at Kennedy High School.

The club was formed so that students experiencing issues regarding sexual orientation and gender identity would have a venue where they could talk about their challenges with like-minded friends in a risk-free environment. They were expecting not to be judged for their lifestyle, and that they still wanted to support the team spirit at Kennedy High School.

Not all Kennedy High School students felt the same way about the LGBTQIA club. The high school football players tore down the club's team spirit banners at one of the football games. Their taunts and jeers encouraged other students also to taunt the members of the club.

Dilemma

The principal now has a situation on his hands where one group of students has bullied another group. In all likelihood the coach, who is in effect the teacher sponsor for the football team, has modeled the bullying for his players by stating but he doesn't want the support of gay students.

The football coach used this term and others that were more derogatory in speaking to the teacher sponsor of the LGBTQIA club. This teacher sponsor and her club members felt unsafe at the football stadium, and they stayed together in a large group too to minimize the possibility of emotional and physical assault.

The principal seems to be siding with the football coach, insinuating that team spirit comes only in one form, and that is through the football team.

The teacher sponsor wants to know what Principal Miller has to say about the LGBTQIA club attendance at school dances like Homecoming and the Prom because the club is prepared to involve an outside agency if they are excluded from school activities.

Questions for Discussion

1. Why would it be appropriate to approve the LGBTQIA club charter?
2. Did the LGBTQIA club have the right to post banners at the football stadium bearing the gay pride flag? Why or why not?
3. How should the principal handle the actions of the football coach and the players on the football team? Should there be consequences for their behavior, and, if so, what should those consequences be?

4. Should Kennedy High School's LGBTQIA students be allowed to go to dances together? What would happen if they mixed with other students? What would happen if they had their own dances?
5. What rights do LGBTQIA students have for protection against bullying? Should they have separate rights that protect them? Defend your answer.
6. Is there such a thing as an LGBTQIA school? Would it even be a good thing to do? Why or why not?

CASE STUDY: *WHO ARE OUR STUDENTS?*
URBAN HIGH SCHOOL GRADES 9–12
EQUITY AND CULTURAL RESPONSIVENESS, 3B
ETHICS AND PROFESSIONAL NORMS, 2A

Background

Jess Jenkins came to the principalship after extensive work in counseling. She began her professional career as a social worker, and then she transitioned to the classroom as a special education teacher. When she went back to school for her master's degree, she pursued clinical psychology and counseling.

That's when she discovered that she had a real heart for school administration.

As a principal, Jess Jenkins knew how to care for her faculty and staff, but she was especially concerned about her students. In the past few years, she noticed that the student population seemed different, but she couldn't put her finger on it.

They were still the same great kids, according to the principal, but they came across as more frazzled and less focused.

The principal was reading an article in the National Education Association magazine when she started to make the connection. Students today had very different lives in high school than did their parents or even their teachers. There were more demands on their time, and as a result, the day was often stretched thin with too much to do in too little time.

In addition, whenever the faculty of the principal called parents about a particular child, they always seemed to interrupt the parents at work—or they woke someone up. Some families were working two or three jobs to make ends meet, but there was a rising number of families on welfare in the community as well. Often students worked part-time jobs to help their families live from month to month.

As a result, the demands on the students and their time increased. Dinners consisted of fast food, eaten on the run to an after school job or to whatever activity was scheduled that day. When the students came home for the night, they were exhausted, but still had four hours of homework ahead of them.

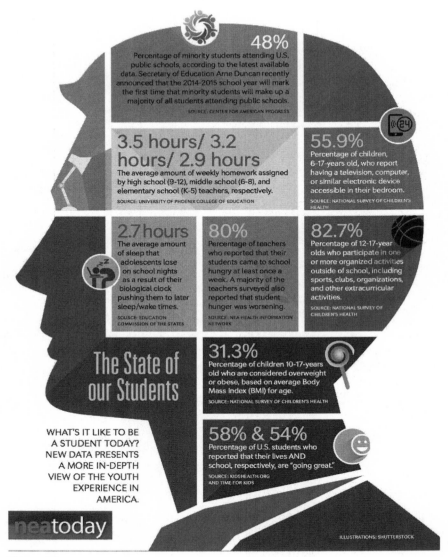

48%

Percentage of minority students attending U.S. public schools, according to the latest available data. Secretary of Education Arne Duncan recently announced that the 2014-2015 school year will mark the first time that minority students will make up a majority of all students attending public schools.

SOURCE: CENTER FOR AMERICAN PROGRESS

3.5 hours/ 3.2 hours/ 2.9 hours

The average amount of weekly homework assigned by high school (9-12), middle school (6-8), and elementary school (K-5) teachers, respectively.

SOURCE: UNIVERSITY OF PHOENIX COLLEGE OF EDUCATION

55.9%

Percentage of children, 6-17-years old, who report having a television, computer, or similar electronic device accessible in their bedroom.

SOURCE: NATIONAL SURVEY OF CHILDREN'S HEALTH

2.7 hours

The average amount of sleep that adolescents lose on school nights as a result of their biological clock pushing them to later sleep/wake times.

SOURCE: EDUCATION COMMISSION OF THE STATES

80%

Percentage of teachers who reported that their students came to school hungry at least once a week. A majority of the teachers surveyed also reported that student hunger was worsening.

SOURCE: NEA HEALTH INFORMATION NETWORK

82.7%

Percentage of 12-17-year olds who participate in one or more organized activities outside of school, including sports, clubs, organizations, and other extracurricular activities.

SOURCE: NATIONAL SURVEY OF CHILDREN'S HEALTH

The State of our Students

31.3%

Percentage of children 10-17-years old who are considered overweight or obese, based on average Body Mass Index (BMI) for age.

SOURCE: NATIONAL SURVEY OF CHILDREN'S HEALTH

WHAT'S IT LIKE TO BE A STUDENT TODAY? NEW DATA PRESENTS A MORE IN-DEPTH VIEW OF THE YOUTH EXPERIENCE IN AMERICA.

58% & 54%

Percentage of U.S. students who reported that their lives AND school, respectively, are "going great."

SOURCE: KIDSHEALTH.ORG AND TIME FOR KIDS

neatoday

ILLUSTRATIONS: SHUTTERSTOCK

Figure 2.1 "What's It Like to Be a Student Today?" *NEA Today* (online), posted October 7, 2014. Reproduced with permission from Cindy Long. Color infographic available from neatoday.org

After reading the article and looking at the infographic shown in figure 2.1, the principal wondered what the statistics at her own school would look like.

"I want to find out who our students are," she told her administrative team. "Let's find out what's really going on."

The teachers, administrators, and counselors distributed surveys among students and collected part of the requested information, illustrated by table 2.1. Principal Jenkins distributed the resulting data at a faculty meeting, asking the teachers to look it over before discussing as a group.

Table 2.1   Principal Jenkin's faculty meeting handout (sample data).

	This year	*1 year ago*	*2 years ago*	*3 years ago*
Percent of minority students	62	57	54	49
Dropout rate	34	28	26	24
Average hours of homework assigned per week	4.0	2.9	3.7	3.5
Percent of students enrolled in advanced classes	11	14	17	22
Percent of students identified as overweight	37	31	30	34
Percent of students who own or have access to a handheld electronic device	62	57	55	52
Average amount of sleep per night	5.2	5.8	6.1	6.5
Percent of students with jobs after school/on weekends	62	35	32	36
Percent of students in extracurricular activities	11	24	29	35

Issue

The principal at an urban high school has been looking at national data trends regarding high school students. This, in turn, led her to wonder where here students were performing compared to national norms.

In short, students were doing more, resting less, and getting further behind. There was clearly less time for students to take care of themselves, and they had had more demands from school and from their families.

High school wasn't easy.

Even the families were suffering more because of economic depression.

Dilemma

Now that the principal has gathered the data for her campus, she shared it with her faculty. She asked them to compare the campus trends to the national trends. Then they were to make recommendations for how to support the students and their families.

The information presented showed a longitudinal picture of students' lives. Students had more to do and yet were less active than ever before.

"How can we educate the whole child?" asked the principal of her faculty. "What can we do about this?"

Questions for Discussion

1. What areas of students' lives are within the school's control to change? Why is it important to understand this? How can this understanding help this issue be addressed?
2. What should the school be most concerned about, and why?
3. What can the school do to decrease the dropout rate?
4. How important is the obesity rate in education?
5. What is the correlation between the reduced enrollment in advanced classes, the increase in after-school jobs and the dropout rates?

Chapter 3

Cultural Competence and Equality for Quality Education

CASE STUDY: *EQUITABLE SUSPENSION*
URBAN HIGH SCHOOL GRADES 9–12
MEANINGFUL ENGAGEMENT OF FAMILIES AND COMMUNITY, 8A, C
EQUITY AND CULTURAL RESPONSIVENESS, 3A

Background

Mr. David Charles was the principal at King High School, a large urban campus in a big city. Mr. Charles had been the principal at this campus for the past nine years. During that time, he had seen a notable increase in the number of student aggressions on campus, including bullying, fighting, and assaults. A similar increase had been documented by all of the other schools in the school district.

In order to deal with the increase in disruptive behaviors, the district had taken a zero tolerance approach to bullying, fighting, and assaults. The new district policy was to mete out the same consequences for every student involved in an incident regardless of who started it or who finished it. The only situation in which all parties would not receive the same consequence was if the student was in special education and had a behavior intervention plan or if the student was a victim of bullying.

Because of confidentiality, administrators were not permitted to discuss the consequences with anyone but the student and the student's guardian.

Campuses were not allowed to suspend a student for more than ten days total during any school year, because any more time away from instruction would severely impact a student's ability to learn the material for the year.

In an effort to help his faculty understand the changes in behaviors at King High School, Mr. Charles has provided targeted staff development at the

27

beginning of each school year regarding dealing with bullies and reducing fights on campus.

Every year discipline referrals were documented at the campus level, and then they were reported to the district and to the state. Although the discipline data were not saved from year to year, King High School had saved its summary data from the past three years to observe and analyze trends in behavior infractions and disciplinary actions.

King High School, under Mr. Charles's leadership, felts it had made progress in the past several years by reducing the number of suspensions and expulsions. The campus had also seen evidence that the same 15 percent of the student body was the most disruptive. The other 85 percent of the student body commit no infractions or very minor infractions.

Jamaal Terrell was a seventeen-year-old sophomore. He was also an African American student. Although his previous infractions included allegedly bringing a BB gun to school (there were no witnesses), fighting during lunch, and vandalizing the boys' restroom, this was a new school year, so Jamaal began the year with a clean slate and no behavior infractions. Like every student at King, Jamaal started the year fresh, with no assumptions about his negative behavior choices.

By the end of the first six weeks, however, Jamaal had been written up for bullying another student who was also African American, and he had been in two fights, neither of which resulted in physical harm to either party. The first fight was between Jamaal and a Hispanic student, and the second fight was between Jamaal and another African American student.

Jamaal was suspended from school for two days due to bullying, and he was suspended for three days each time he had been fighting.

Now Jamaal had been caught fighting again. During the sophomore lunch, the two assistant principals and one of the coaches broke up a fight between Jamaal and another boy. Jamaal's friends, DeAndre and Tyrone, were present and reportedly incited the fight.

Now Jamaal and Connor were each sitting in one of the assistant principals' offices and holding an ice pack to the quickly swelling areas on their faces. The assistant principals questioned the boys individually about the fight. They wanted to know who started it and what the fight was about.

That's when Mr. Charles came to see what had happened.

"It doesn't matter who started the fight or who ended the fight. They are both suspended," he told his assistants. "We have a zero tolerance policy in our district, and King High School supports that policy. Suspend them both, same amount of time."

When the school administration called Connor's mom, she said she would come and pick him up, and she also requested her son's school assignments for the next three days. "There's no way that boy is going to sit at home with nothing to do for the next three days," she said to the assistant principal. If you have to, feel free to double his assignments. I want him busy the entire time so that he's happy to get back to school on the fourth day."

When the assistant principal called Jamaal's mother, she said to go ahead and send him home. She would take care of everything from there.

Mr. Charles followed up the next day with the assistant principals to make sure both boys had been suspended according to district policy. The assistant principals affirmed that both boys had been suspended for three days.

Principal Charles was completely surprised when, on the fourth day, it was not Jamaal who returned to school, but rather, his mother. She had come to tell the principal that she was seeking legal relief regarding Jamaal's suspension. Mrs. Terrell informed the principal that her son was now suffering from pain, humiliation, human mistreatment, and racial discrimination as a result of the suspension. He could not return to school because of the extreme embarrassment.

Furthermore, Mrs. Terrell informed the principal that she intended to sue him as well for racial discrimination against her son.

"You are always picking on my boy," she said. "You look for things to find wrong about him so you can send him home. And it's all because he's black. I know you don't send the white kids home on suspension. It's only the black kids, like my Jamaal. It's obvious that you hate black kids. What you did is not fair. You didn't suspend the other boys who had been in the fight, only my son."

Mr. Charles asked her where Mrs. Terrell had gotten her information from.

"My son told me all about it," she said. "Jamaal told me the other boy, the one who started the fight, was a white kid, and he didn't have any consequence. At least, he was not suspended. Only Jamaal got suspended, which seems to be happening a whole lot."

Issue

Jamaal Terrell has a history of aggressive behavior at King High School. As a freshman in the previous year, Jamaal had several incidents, and as a result was suspended each time. This year as a sophomore, Jamaal had also been suspended three times so far, for a total of eight days. His list of offenses included bullying and fighting.

After his most recent fight with another student, Jamaal was suspended again this time for three days. The other student was white. The fight was incited by two other black students, both of whom are friends with Jamaal.

Jamaal's mother was furious that her son had been suspended again, and she planned to sue the principal and the school district because of the pain and humiliation her son experienced with each suspension.

Dilemma

Some of the students, about 15 percent, at King High School are considered repeat offenders when it comes to bad behavior. Their behavior infractions do not accrue year after year; each year, the students begin with a clean slate. This year, however, Jamaal had already committed several serious infractions.

Jamaal has been suspended for a total of eleven days, which exceeds the state allowance for instructional days away from the campus.

In addition, Jamaal's mother Mrs. Terrell wants to sue the school principal and school district because of her son's suffering. She feels as though her son is being persecuted because he is black. She claims that the other student involved in the last fight did not receive consequences that were as severe as her son's. Therefore, the school principal has discriminated against her child racially.

She is seeking damages of $100,000.

Questions for Discussion

1. Would it make a difference if Principal Charles was black? Why or why not? What if Connor was black?
2. Should Mr. Charles show the suspension documentation to Mrs. Terrell? Why or why not?
3. The number of days that Jamaal has been suspended exceeded ten, which is the maximum amount allowed. What should the administration do?
4. Should there be any consequences for DeAndre and Tyrone? Why or why not? If there are consequences, what should they be?
5. Would you have made Jamaal's punishment progressive, meaning that each time he committed an infraction, you increased the penalty? Why or why not?
6. How can Mr. Charles involve parents and the community in their behavior management at King High School?

CASE STUDY: *LOCKER ROOM BULLIES*
RURAL MIDDLE SCHOOL GRADES PK–5
EQUITY AND CULTURAL RESPONSIVENESS, 3A, B

Background

Eighth grader Ben Steinberg just moved to Rockcliff Middle School from a much larger metropolitan area. His parents wanted their son to experience life in the suburbs, and they chose the Rockcliff Community for Ben to complete his middle and high school years.

"Be active in as many things as you can," they told Ben. "You'll get good experiences that you'll never forget. They'll be with you a lifetime."

Truer words were never spoken.

Ben discovered on his first day of class that he was probably the only Orthodox Jew in the entire school. Apparently no one had seen a yarmulke, or skullcap, before. As he walked down the halls, he received stares and some of the students pointed and giggled at the cap that covered the top of his head.

At lunch, one of the students asked, "Are you going bald or what? What's that hat for? Couldn't you afford a real one that covered your whole head?"

By the end of his first day at school, Ben felt horrible. Even one of his teachers told him that he had to remove his hat in public places, including the classroom. Ben had been too tired to argue, and he removed the kippah and placed it inside a textbook.

He said nothing to his parents until the end of the week, when his father had returned from a business trip.

On Monday morning, Mr. Stein was in the principal's office immediately after the start of school. "Mr. Beckman, are you Jewish?" he asked.

Principal Tobias Beckman said that although he was not of that faith, he certainly wanted to know what was on Mr. Stein's mind. He noticed that Mr. Stein wore a small cap similar to his son's.

"Ah, it's okay," said Mr. Stein. "No one's perfect. But my Ben has been having problems here in your school. He's being bullied."

Mr. Stein explained the situation, and then wrapped up the conversation. "So you see, Mr. Beckman, we are extremely traditional in my family, and we wear our kippahs out of respect for our God. Doing so shows that we understand our place in relation to him. I would like my son to be respected for his choice to wear the kippah in public, especially here in your school."

The principal assured Mr. Stein that he would look into the matter.

That afternoon, Principal Beckman held a faculty meeting. During one portion of the meeting, he noted that he had seen an increase in bullying on the campus, and he wanted the teachers to step in if they saw any bullying activities going on. He also explained why the new student Ben Stein wore a kippah, and how important it was to him. He asked the faculty to support and respect the student's decision to wear the skullcap.

The interest in Ben's kippah began to wear down and fade away after a few weeks, thanks to some of the teachers helping their students staying more focused on learning tasks and less on cultural differences. The more his classmates learned to respect Ben, the more they liked him.

The only place Ben still had difficulty was with the football team. The coach, Don Sinclair, didn't like the idea of Ben wearing his kippah under the football helmet, but the skullcap didn't interfere with football so he shrugged and let it go. He figured he'd let the team handle it in the locker room. They always hazed the newest members of the team to "break them in" and create a brotherhood of sorts, and they'd figure out what to do with Ben.

Thursday afternoon after practice, the players went into the locker room to change out of their pads and uniforms. As they were tossing their uniforms in the team's laundry basket, they noticed Ben had gone to the showers. He left his skullcap on his locker shelf.

One of the boys grabbed the cap and began hurling it around the room like a Frisbee. Several teammates joined in the fun.

When Ben came back from the shower, he saw what was going on, and he lunged for his kippah. A game of keep-away ensued, and the football players called Ben names and warned him of what they might do to him if he didn't do whatever the other players told him to do.

In a final attempt to grab his kippah and put it back on his head, Ben jumped up into the air. When he landed, he lost his footing on the wet concrete floor. As Ben fell, he hit his head on the metal bench, and a gash opened up, pouring out blood. The players stopped the game, frozen in place. Finally, Arnie Gomez rushed forward, and he held a towel against the gash to stop or at least slow down the bleeding.

"Call the coach!" he yelled.

Coach Sinclair rushed into the locker room, with the principal right on his heels.

"I think you're going to need an ambulance, sir," said Arnie. "Ben probably should get stitches for this."

Coach looked around the locker room, trying to figure out what had happened.

As he dialed on his mobile phone, Principal Beckman looked at the coach and then at his son.

"Hey man, it's all in good fun," said Jonathan Sinclair, the football team captain. "You didn't really think we were trying to kill him, did you?"

Issue

New student Ben Stein is being bullied because of his decision to wear his kippah, a religious skullcap, in school. His dad comes to school to speak to the principal about the situation, and Principal Beckman assures Mr. Stein the bullying will stop. While the bullying does improve in the classrooms, Ben still faces bullying in the locker room after football practice. The bullying, also called hazing, is being meted out at the direction of the football captain, who is also the coach's son.

Dilemma

The Rockcliff Middle School football coach is aware that a "certain amount" of hazing takes place in the locker room, and he's willing to allow that so the team forms a "brotherhood." This behavior has been standard practice for a long time, and the coach sees no reason for it to stop.

While Ben is showering, the players grab his kippah and toss it around the room. When Ben returns to the locker room and tries to grab his skullcap, he slips, falls, and hits his head. He will need immediate medical care.

Questions for Discussion

1. Should Mr. Beckman call 911 or the parents first? Why?
2. How appropriate would it have been to ban Ben from wearing the kippah at school?
3. Is the coach responsible for the incident in the locker room? Why or why not?
4. Should Jonathan Sinclair receive any consequences for Ben's injury?
5. What would be different if the new student had been a Sikh or a Muslim? What if he had been a Rastafarian?

CASE STUDY: *BETTER RATINGS*
URBAN MIDDLE SCHOOL GRADES 6–8
EQUITY AND CULTURAL RESPONSIVENESS, 3F, G
COMMUNITY OF CARE AND SUPPORT FOR STUDENTS, 5E

Background

Victor Molina had been a middle school teacher for more than a decade, and the one thing he knew was that he wanted to be a middle school principal. He was one of those educators who thrived on being with middle school kids. Every day with them was different, because they seemed to have one foot in childhood and the other in their teen years.

When the public school system placed Mr. Molina at Ace Middle School in the center of the metroplex, the new principal was excited beyond belief. He would finally become instrumental in making some of the changes he knew needed to happen if middle school students were going to be successful.

One of these areas was bullying. Mr. Molina had seen the effects of bullying with his own eyes. Middle schoolers were especially notorious about bullying in their preteen years, and often the bullying devastated the victim and those around him or her, sometimes driving the victim to suicide.

The public school system was required to report all incidents of bullying to the state's education agency. The state gathered the self-reported data and announced safety ratings of every school based on the number of bullying incidents. The only accountability in the system was to turn in the number of incidents on or before the due date.

Mr. Molina had just come from a meeting with the other secondary principals, where they reviewed the data from past year's bullying reports. Overall, the district had done well in reducing the number of bullying incidents. It was down 24 percent from the previous year. All of the principals clapped each other on the backs, congratulating their peers on a job well done.

Mr. Molina looked forward to being part of the celebration next year. He knew from the day's training that at least half of all students reported having been bullied at some point in school, and almost two out of every ten kids had been bullied electronically. Mr. Molina began to wonder about the students back at Ace. How many of them had been bullied?

Then he considered the district's reported numbers regarding bullying. The campuses had cut the bullying in half, according to what he had learned today. That was impressive work, and he made a mental note to contact some of his colleagues to find out what they were doing right to protect kids and keep them safe from bullying.

Principal Molina wanted to do more than create a no-tolerance policy regarding bullying or to suspend students for bullying each other, whether it was through physical bullying or cyberbullying. During the academic year, Mr. Molina worked with his teachers and counselors on developing bullying prevention programs based on mutual respect for each other. Together, they involved the parents and community at large, and they also met with the cafeteria workers and the bus drivers to come up with plans that could really help children who were often targeted as bullies. Mr. Molina and his faculty collected data from each of the incidents, and noticed some interesting trends.

When the teachers knew what to look for, they were able to consistently spot bullying and intervene on the behalf of the victims. They often didn't see the bullying itself, but they began to notice the effects of bullying, such as changes in behavior. A boy who had been outgoing and charismatic may become more reticent in an attempt to blend into his surroundings. A girl who has begun cutting herself in an attempt to over the pain and shame of being bullied may wear long sleeves on the hottest of days.

The faculty referred students to the counselors, and, slowly, the issue of bullying was brought out into the open.

It was hard to believe, but the data that the Ace Middle School team collected indicated that the bullying rate on the campus was a whopping 47 percent. Like the national statistics they had reviewed, the faculty discovered that almost half the students at Ace had been bullied that year.

When Mr. Molina broke down the data, he discovered that 21 percent of the bullying was through electronic devices. The rest of the bullying was split evenly, with 40 percent being verbal attacks and 40 percent being physical attacks, including touching, pinching, pulling, and pushing. Fifteen percent of the bullying happened in the school cafeteria, and another 32 percent took place on the buses. Ten percent of the bullying took place in the halls, but the principal was astounded to learn that the rest of the bullying occurred in the classroom, right in front of the teachers.

The principal was pleased that his team had collected such great data. He felt that they could use this as a springboard to build an effective antibullying program.

Mr. Molina met for lunch with his colleagues.

"Hey, how's your bullying data looking?" asked Mr. Molina. "I'm curious because we've collected ours, and although the numbers are high, I think we've got a way to make a difference and create an effective antibullying plan." Then he talked about some of the trends his campus had seen.

"Geez, you did all that work?" asked one of the other principals. "What for?"

"Yeah, no kidding," said another one. "Haven't you already got enough work to do without stirring up trouble and making the rest of us look bad?"

"What are you talking about?" said Mr. Molina.

"We don't turn in real numbers. We'd all get fired. We just change them up a little."

Issue

Principal Victor Molina has made a concerted effort to gather honest data regarding bullying at his campus. Based on the data he's collected, his campus data closely mimic the national averages.

Disappointed in how high his numbers are compared to the numbers at his colleagues' campuses, Mr. Molina at least feels as though he knows which areas to concentrate on in building his antibullying program.

The other principals reveal that they lie about their data so that their campuses—and the school system—do not look bad in the eyes of the community.

Dilemma

The new middle school principal has been asked to falsify a data report by omitting information that he is legally required to include. Omitting the information will place his school in a better light for antibullying statistics, and it likely also means that his contract as principal will be renewed.

Revealing the real truth about bullying at the middle school campus means that the district will be in peril of losing its stellar rating with the state education agency, the district will lose its rating, and the principal may lose his job.

The other principals provide encouragement, telling him that they all "doctor" the data. So they look better.

Questions for Discussion

1. What about Mr. Molina's approach to creating an antibullying program is appropriate?
2. What type of professional development should the Ace Middle School teachers receive?
3. How can Ace Middle School and the school system better protect children?
4. What's the problem with self-reporting for accountability?
5. Should Mr. Molina report what he has learned from his colleagues about their campus antibullying data?
6. What data should Mr. Molina report?

CASE STUDY: *PLANNING FOR IT*
RURAL HIGH SCHOOL
EQUITY AND CULTURAL RESPONSIVENESS, 3C
MEANINGFUL ENGAGEMENT OF FAMILIES AND COMMUNITY, 8B

Background

In the first year, Principal Jamila Omar was surprised to see the graduation rates for her campus. Only 85 percent of her seniors were completing their courses of study and graduating from high school. She had figured that in a rural community, there would be much more emphasis on getting that high school diploma and moving on to other opportunities.

When she reviewed the plans on which the seniors were graduating, she was equally surprised to see how few of seniors were graduating on the advanced plan recommended by the state. Many students were opting for the far less rigorous foundation plan. Judging by the signatures on some of the plans, the counselors, parents, students, and even the former principal agreed with decisions being made.

The principal wanted to see an increase in the numbers of students taking the recommended and advanced graduation plans. It seemed to her that her first step would be to talk to the incoming freshmen about the paths choices that lie before them.

When she addressed the freshmen group in the auditorium, she discovered that many of the students didn't even realize they needed a plan, or that they didn't get promoted from year to year in high like they had been in elementary and middle schools. As she explained earning credits for classes, the principal realized that she had a considerable amount of work ahead of her (see table 3.1).

Table 3.1 Principal Omar's graduation plan findings (sample data).

	Foundation Plan	Recommended Plan	Advanced Plan
Percentage of Students Graduating in 2017	73	21	6
Percentage of Students Graduating in 2016	68	31	1
Percentage of Students Graduating in 2016	55	45	10
Percentage of Students Graduating in 2016	52	38	10

That was just the beginning. As Principal Omar met with the sophomores and then the juniors, she discovered by show of hands that few of them had personal graduation plans. Less than half the students raised their hands when asked if they had a plan.

"Oh we only do those if the student or his parents ask," said one of the counselors. "Or if they are in special education. We always do one for those kids. But anything else is just extra work."

"And which parents ask for those plans?" asked the principal.

"Well, usually, it's the parents of kids who are going on to college. Those are really the only ones who are interested in seeing a plan," said the counselor. "You know, the ones who can afford it. The rest of the graduates just get job in town, or whatever."

"What about the students who want to go to college but have no idea how to prepare for it because they were never encouraged?" asked the principal.

"Oh, we pretty much know who is college material and who is not," said the counselor.

The principal couldn't believe what she was hearing. How many students had been denied the opportunity to pursue higher education?

How many students were denied a future they didn't even know existed?

Issue

When the new principal took over the leadership of the high school campus in a rural community, she discovered that few students graduated on the advanced degree plan, and even fewer had a personal graduation plan that showed them each step in their path toward getting a high school diploma and matriculating in a college or university.

The counselor had a laissez-faire attitude about providing students with the information needed. In fact, she did the minimum required by federal law, making sure that special education students had graduation plans. She also made them up for parents requesting them for their children, but that was it.

High School Students with Personal Graduation Plans

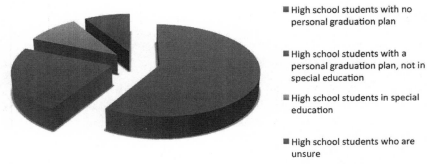

■ High school students with no personal graduation plan

■ High school students with a personal graduation plan, not in special education

■ High school students in special education

■ High school students who are unsure

Figure 3.1   Infographic of Principal Omar's graduation plan findings (sample data).

Dilemma

Students at this rural high school have been denied the opportunity to advance their education because the counselor has not shown them how credits work or what's involved in a high school graduation plan.

Her rationale has been that she knows who is college material and who is not. Therefore, she plans with students accordingly. When parents request personal graduation plans, or when federal law requires them, she provides them.

As a result, few students graduate having taken more rigorous courses. The graduation rate is only 85 percent.

The principal is ready to take action.

Questions for Discussion

1. How can the principal get parents interested in personal graduation plans and more advanced coursework for their children?
2. How can the students be encouraged to attempt more rigorous programs of study?
3. What other factors might influence the graduation plans for high school students? And why are they important for understanding your school?
4. How can the dropout rate be reduced?
5. What action does the principal need to take in regard to the counselor's attitude about personal graduation plans?

Chapter 4

Curriculum and Instruction

CASE STUDY: *METACOGNITION FOR HIGH SCHOOL*
SUBURBAN HIGH SCHOOL GRADES 9–12
CURRICULUM, INSTRUCTION, AND ASSESSMENT, 4C
SCHOOL IMPROVEMENT, 10D

Background

Jose Garcia knew that his high school faculty was set in its ways, and several members were determined to see the next initiative in education go down in flames and fail. Enchanted Elm High School was a large campus in an established neighborhood of the suburbs.

With a 26:1 student ratio, there were 115 teachers in the faculty. All of them were meeting in the library with the principal. Today's topic was a discussion about improving instruction. Student achievement at Elms High School was good, but the school had really moved forward in several years. Principal Garcia was worried that unless they realigned their teaching methods, student achievement might actually slip backward.

The district was committed to utilizing the metacognition research from John Hattie, but several of the teachers at the high school were adamant about not changing their instructional approach. The teachers had just completed a group work assignment requiring them to brainstorm the different teaching strategies used in their discipline.

Some of the strategies reported included the following:

- Sidecoaching
- Lecture and note-taking
- Whole language and process writing
- Use of PowerPoint

- Use of other visual aids
- Explicit vocabulary instruction
- Interactive notebooks
- Hands-on experiments
- Reenactments
- Reading/answering questions
- Reading/writing essays
- Cooperative learning
- Class discussion
- Practice/rehearsal

Then the principal showed the teachers a "Learning Pyramid" graph (represented by figure 4.1) and asked them where along the "pyramid" their preferred strategies would reside.

The groups of teachers looked at the learning pyramid.

Principal Garcia knew the information would not be well received by some of the teachers. The strategies they used fell in some of the lowest student retention rates. Many of the Enchanted Elms teachers had been teaching for decades. They didn't appreciate anyone telling them they had to change their instructional methods, regardless of how outdated or possibly ineffective those methods were.

"But I have always taught this way," said Mrs. Meyers. "My lectures have been refined over the years, and I present only the best information to students. The students learn note-taking and organizational skills, and that's something they don't get anywhere else. My students always do fine. I've put a lot of work into my teaching. I don't see why I am being forced to change."

"Oh sure, you just lecture—no reason to change there," said Mr. Bailey, one of the teachers. "I always add visual demonstrations."

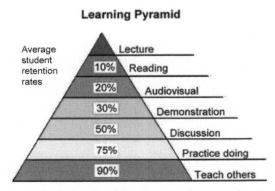

Figure 4.1 "The Learning Pyramid." Adapted from the National Training Laboratory in Bethel, Main.

"Well, of course you do," said Mrs. Meyers. "You teach science, Mr. Bailey. I'd say it's pretty easy to include a demonstration. Try demonstrations in reading literature, sometime. My method has worked great for years. I even assign summer reading and writing projects before the students come to my class. They have all that time before school starts, so there's no reason to waste those months."

She continued to point out that some of the research they had learned from John Hattie's work validated her summer assignments.

"Summer vacation is pretty much a complete waste of time. Hattie said so. That's why I've always given out summer assignments," said Mrs. Meyers.

Principal Garcia said, "Yes, you are right about long summer vacations. Let's look at those efforts that make the greatest impact on student achievement." Then he showed his next slide, which is depicted in Figure 4.2.

Mrs. Meyers looked at the screen and snorted. "I'm telling you, I'm not changing what I'm doing. I don't need tenth graders teaching each other incorrect information, and I'm not about to develop relationships with students and get all touchy feely with their emotional sides. And the students already get feedback. It's called a grade."

Several of the teachers in her department applauded Mrs. Meyers for taking a stand.

Issue

The high school principal knew that his teachers were going to have to adjust their teachers and make changes in the classroom if student achievement was going to continue growing at Enchanted Elms High School.

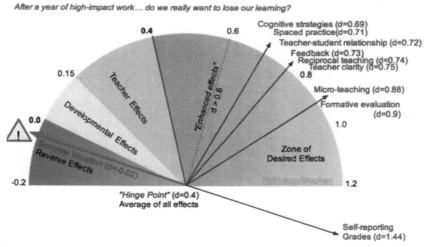

Figure 4.2 Reproduced with permission from John Hattie (2012). Original in color.

The district adopted the research of John Hattie, and visible learning was something most teachers were excited about, especially at the elementary and middle school levels.

The high school teachers were skeptical, thinking it one more trend in education that would come and hopefully go.

The principal need to get the teachers to change their minds.

Dilemma

The principal guided the large faculty through several exercises designed to get them talking about classroom practices. He wanted the teachers to reflect on how they delivered instruction, including the methods used.

Some of the teachers insisted that what they had been doing for decades was actually quite effective, and there was no reason to change.

One teacher in particular stood her ground. When she refused to consider any new instructional strategies, many of the teachers in her department applauded her.

The principal was worried that this teacher would develop a following and the entire department would refuse to try newer instructional methods that would be more effective.

Questions for Discussion

1. Which of the strategies reported by the teachers are of least effect? Which show the most promise for improved student achievement?
2. Mrs. Meyers assigns summer school homework for her incoming students. How can the assignments be made more effective, according to Hattie's research?
3. How can the principal help the teachers implement strategies from the zone of desired effect?
4. What are the principal's next steps with Mrs. Meyers and her department? Why?
5. What would you do if Mrs. Meyers continued to refuse changing her instructional approach?

CASE STUDY: *NEW MATH*
RURAL MIDDLE SCHOOL GRADES 6–8
CURRICULUM, INSTRUCTION, AND ASSESSMENT, 4B

Background

Teaching Algebra in high school can be a difficult assignment. Not only does the teacher have to be able to explain algebraic concepts to students who may not be ready for abstract thinking, but the teacher must also be able to keep the attention of teenagers who would rather do anything except mathematics.

Algebra teacher Tony Riddle understood quite well but the only way the students would listen to his instruction or attempt to do any of the math would be if he made it interesting enough for the students. Armed with only a white board and the algebra book, Mr. Riddle did the best he could with what he had.

Liesel Johnson, the principal at Meadow Crest Middle School, had visited Mr. Riddle's classroom several times, and each time she commented about this discipline management. The students were not paying attention to the lesson and Mr. Riddle was not doing anything to keep his students interested and engaged in the algebra lesson.

To make sure that the incident was not an isolated case, Mr. Johnson visited several of Mr. Riddle's classes. She saw similar behaviors in each class she visited, regardless of the time of day.

"You have behavior problems in your classroom because your lessons are boring and the students see no connection between algebra and the real world. Until you can help them see that connection, you will always have behavior problems and your students will not listen to you," the principal told the algebra teacher.

Mr. Little requested to attend professional development on how to engage students in algebra and help them see real-world connections. His requests were denied based on the campus having a little additional monies for professional development, and the fact that Mr. Riddle was a newer teacher.

Mr. Riddle also asked to be allowed to observe instruction and some of the other algebra teachers' classrooms. "I hear them talking about their lesson plans, But I would like to see them in action," said Mr. Riddle. "I think that would help me figure out how to bridge the gap."

The principal again denied his request, saying that she could not afford to have a substitute in Mr. Riddle's classroom while he was off someplace else. She needed him in his classroom teaching.

Principal Johnson left Mr. Riddle with a final warning. "If you cannot get your classroom management in check, I may have no recourse but to recommend that your contract not be renewed."

Mr. Riddle had always wanted to be a teacher; the possibility of having his profession stripped from him was a cruel blow. He spent the weekend devising away to get his students interested and math problems he was trying to explain. Mr. Justin decided that two things would grab his students' attention: drugs and sex.

Therefore, he devised algebraic problems involving either drugs or sex. When Mr. Riddle used the problems in his first-period class, he was ecstatic with the outcome. He had caught his students' attention, and all it took was a simple problem like this:

> Tony can send five texts and three nudes in nineteen minutes. He could also send three texts and one nude in nine minutes. How long would it take him to send one text and one nude?

Students who had formerly wanted nothing to do with algebra were now attempting the problems. In many cases, they were even coming up with the correct answers. It seemed as though Mr. Riddle had found a way to connect algebra to the real world.

Unfortunately, for Mr. Riddle, the parents saw the algebra problems their children brought home. They were outraged. The Algebra teacher was endorsing illicit and illegal behaviors like abusing drugs and sexting digital pornography.

One of the parents took a photograph of the questions Mr. Riddle had prepared for homework, and the parent posted the picture of these questions on a social media page. Other parents saw the content, and they too were alarmed how a teacher at the high school would think it's okay for students to practice with problems like these. Mr. Riddle saw some of the comments, and he jumped into the conversation, explaining that this was the world his students lived in.

"Not in my house," wrote one of the parents.

Another parent added but hardly approved teaching minor students about drugs and sex.

One of the parents contacted Principal Stevens the next morning. He demanded that his daughter be placed in a different algebra class.

"I do not want her with the teachers that is a pervert and does not know boundaries in working with children," said the parent.

Principal Stevens assured the parent that his daughter would be moved to another classroom. Several other messages came in for the principal next day, and every one of them was a transfer request. Although Mr. Riddle found a way to engage the students, their parents did not want their children in the sort of classroom environment the algebra teacher was offering.

Several of the parents demanded to know what other lapses in judgment Mr. Riddle might have had, but the principal refused to honor their requests.

Issue

Tony Riddle is a new teacher at the middle school. He has been having difficulty getting and holding his students' attention trying to teach algebra. His requests for professional development have repeatedly been turned down, so in desperation, the math teacher has crafted algebra problems centered in drugs and sexting.

Although he gained his students' attention, he lost the respect of the parents. They are now demanding that their children no longer have class with Mr. Riddle.

Dilemma

Math teacher Tony Riddle has been using problems about drugs and sex thing to teach algebraic concepts in class. Because both activities are illegal, they're inappropriate topics for the classroom, especially one full of minor students.

The parents want their children removed from his classroom, and they want to know what other infractions Mr. Riddle has faced in the past. In short, they want to know if he is not repeatedly making the same offenses over and over and that he is not a sexual predator.

Mr. Riddle has accused the principal of forcing him into this position because he was denied professional development opportunities that could have helped him engage students and keep their attention.

Questions for Discussion

1. What was wrong with the way the teacher got his students' attention? Explain why the math problems were unacceptable.
2. Why should the principal let parents know what is going on with this issue?
3. How should the principal document her interactions with Mr. Riddle, including the request to stop using algebra problems based on illegal activities?
4. The teacher had only basic tools—a whiteboard and a textbook—to teach algebra. How much of the blame lives with the district or the campus?
5. Should the principal take any of the blame because she refused to send the teacher to professional development? What is the problem of withholding professional development from newer teachers?

CASE STUDY: *CHEATERS*
URBAN CHARTER HIGH SCHOOL GRADES 9–12
CURRICULUM, INSTRUCTION, AND ASSESSMENT, 4F

Background

Epiphany Charter High School served students looking for an edge in getting into colleges and universities. The school's curriculum was considered one of the most rigorous programs in the city, and students had to devote considerable time to their studies in order to make the grades they need and score well on college prep exams.

Epiphany Charter was led by Principal Moses Bowie. He was a kind man who wore a serious expression on his face. That expression was there whether he was concerned or joyous. Sometimes the kids joked behind his back and called him Stoneface Bowie.

Mr. Bowie was a devoted principal. He worried about whether his students and his teachers had what they need to be successful in the classroom. He spent a lot of his own money and much of this time in making sure that the technology on campus was as current as it could possibly be.

He was able to combine local technology funds and eRate funding in order to make their technology dollars go further. Unfortunately, the money was never enough and Mr. Bowie still had to be creative when administering the standardized assessments for the state and for college entrance exams.

The high-stakes testing was important because scores could determine whether or not one of the Epiphany Charter students was accepted into college. Part of the school's mission and vision was to find every enrolled student a seat in a college for further education. Mr. Bowie and the faculty felt strongly that the best way out of poverty is through advanced education, and they were intent on making a possibility a reality for their students.

In order to accommodate all of the testing that must take place, Mr. Bowie developed elaborate testing schedules that would permit students to take their tests online over the course of an open window of time rather than on paper on one given day. The testing window for electronic assessments spanned a several week period.

The first group of students took their assessments at the beginning of the testing window. Although they were not allowed to have cell phones or other electronic devices in the testing room, some of the students brought them in anyway and discreetly took screenshots of the assessment questions.

They've posted these screenshots onto a variety of social media sites, here others immediately liked or favorited the posts so they could find them later. Within two hours, the completion of the first assessments, most of the students at Epiphany Charter School had seen the test questions, and we're already discussing the answers to the questions.

Nathan began to post and retweet not only the questions but also the answers.

Mr. Bowie was unaware of the social media fervor surrounding state assessment. There were however others who were monitoring the situation closely.

One such group monitors included the security firm hired by the testing company. The testing company had a contract with the state and guaranteed that all of the testing material and content would be kept confidential until the date of release some six months later or longer. In addition, the high-stakes testing company guaranteed the integrity of the assessments given.

The commitment to integrity and confidentiality prompted the testing company to hire the security monitoring group. It was the job of the security monitoring group to peruse every social media site use by students to watch for test breaches in the form of screenshots, content, and answers to the test questions.

To perform their job, the test security company and monitors searched and trolled through private information on students' social media accounts. Most of the students in question were under the age of eighteen. None of them knew that someone was monitoring their social media pages.

Mr. Bowie did not know it either, until a director from the testing company called him on the phone to make him aware of the situation.

"Mr. Bowie," send the testing company representative, "we have every reason to believe that several of your students have violated the confidentiality policy outlined by our testing company. In addition, we have the names of the faculty and staff who proctored the exams in question. You need to know that we are considering disciplinary action against not only the students but also the teachers. I'm calling you as a courtesy to let you know that we may be taking disciplinary action against you as the principal of the campus."

As well Mr. Bowie was stunned. "How do you even have the right to do this?" he asked.

The testing company representative said, "We have every right to protect our intellectual property. You have to understand that every question on every exam we write costs us $15,000. It's not good business for us to throw out a question just because it is no longer considered secure."

"But you have field questions," said Mr. Bowie. "Use one of those in its place."

"We can't," said the representative. "The field questions have not been properly vetted."

"What happens if the students took a picture on a field question? Does it matter if they've violated the tests security protocol?" asked Principal Bowie.

The representative responded, "I assure you that that was not the case. The questions posted on social media were authentic test questions. As a courtesy you might want to let the parents know that will be contacting them about their children's actions. I have a list of names, addresses, and phone numbers right here if you'd like to take notes."

"How did you get this information," asked Mr. Bowie.

"It's all right there on the social media pages, in the open, like public information," said the testing representative. "It makes it easy to find anybody."

Issue

Like many schools, Tiffany charter school has to be careful with its budget. One of the greatest expenses after salaries is keeping up with modern technology. The principal would like to have more technology available for students on his campus, but the budget goes only so far.

Technology has been great for high-stakes testing, because the assessments are given across a several-week window of time. The students, however, were able to sneak cell phones and other electronic devices into the testing room and take screenshots of exam questions. The exam questions were posted in social media and made public, even though the students and teachers were proctoring the exam had signed confidentiality agreements.

Dilemma

Unbeknownst to the principal, his teachers, students, or their parents, the high-stakes testing company contracted with an outside security agency to monitor all social media platforms for any breaches of test confidentiality. The monitoring company was looking for specific test question and references to test content in particular.

The company found evidence that students cheated on the exam by posting screenshots to their personal social media pages, where other students saved the content for when they took the same exam.

At high-stakes assessment, company representative has called the campus principal as a courtesy to let him know their findings about the breach in test confidentiality and integrity. The company intends to pursue all involved individuals with disciplinary action.

Questions for Discussion

1. What actions steps should the principal take when he finishes his phone call with the high-stakes assessment company director?
2. How should Mr. Bowie tell the parents, who are likely unaware, that an outside agency has been reviewing their children's personal social media accounts?
3. What are the ethical ramifications of trolling through personal information posted by a minor child?
4. If you were the principal at Epiphany Charter High School, what would you tell the teachers who had proctored the exams?
5. What are the ramifications of cheating on a high-stakes assessment? What consequences should the school give to the students who cheated?

Chapter 5

Supportive School Community

CASE STUDY: *YOUTH VIOLENCE*
URBAN HIGH SCHOOL GRADES 9–12
COMMUNITY OF CARE AND SUPPORT FOR STUDENTS, 5A, B

Background

Metro High School was located in a high-crime area of the city. Years ago, people in the community joked that if you didn't have a knife when you went to Metro, they'd give you one at the door so that you'd have a fair chance at defending yourself.

Luis Gonzalez, the Metro High principal, didn't think the joke was the least bit funny. He had become the principal four years ago, just after the previous principal resigned due to an incident that took place on campus. Two rival gangs agreed to fight during the lunch period. Some of the teachers had learned in advance who would be fighting as well as where and what time the fight would take place.

The previous principal said, "Let'em duke it out. That means a few less thugs in the system." Because he refused to stop the fight from happening, he was charged with endangerment of a child and was considered an accomplice to murder when one of the gang members stabbed and fatally wounded another.

When Principal Gonzalez took over the campus, he began to work on the school's image. He had metal detectors installed at the front doors of the building, where he required every student and employee to walk through. The principal himself was there to greet everyone as they entered the building, and it was something he did every single day. He had had 100 percent attendance for the past four years. When he was called to a meeting somewhere else, it was understood that he would be late because he had morning greeting time to take care of first.

The students and faculty hated the procedure at first, because it slowed entry into the building. After a while, however, they began to appreciate the principal's commitment to their safety. The parents and community loved the idea that the high school was a safe haven.

It was important to Principal Gonzalez that his campus be weapon-free. He had seen the data from the Centers for Disease Control, represented by figure 5.1, about students who were threatened at school. Almost 7 percent of students nationwide reported being threatened at school with a weapon of some sort. "At school" meant in the building, at a school event (like the football stadium), or even on a field trip.

Five years ago, 27 percent of Metro High Schools students reported being threatened with a weapon.

Principal Gonzalez had no intention of resting on his laurels. He was equally concerned about other violent behavior on his campus, and he was concerned that the number of incidents was steadily growing.

His administration team presented him with the following information represented by table 5.1.

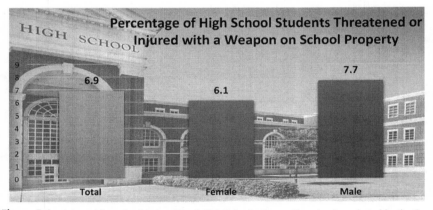

Figure 5.1   Adapted from the "National Youth Risk Behavior Survey Overview" conducted by the Centers for Disease Control (2015). Data and original infographic available on the CDC website (cdc.gov/violenceprevention/).

Table 5.1   Depiction of school-related violence experienced by high school students.

Percent of Students:	2013	2014	2015	2016	2017
Threatened with a weapon	27	19	15	6	1
Caught fighting at school	43	35	26	11	10
Reported being bullied	62	38	22	24	55
Experienced electronic aggression	31	25	21	18	44
Victim of gang violence	57	45	36	21	28

Sample data based on the Youth Risk Behavior Surveillance System surveys conducted by the Centers for Disease Control (cdc.gov/violenceprevention/).

Then they compared it with the data they had for disciplinary action taken, represented by table 5.2.

Table 5.2 Disciplinary action taken in response to school-related violence.

Percentage of Students:	2013	2014	2015	2016	2017
Sent to detention before/after school	27	40	25	22	3
In-school suspension	48	14	10	9	4
Out-of-school suspension	35	7	5	5	2
Sent to alternative center	24	8	5	3	1
Sent to juvenile detention center	12	3	5	2	0

Sample data based on Youth Risk Behavior Surveillance System surveys, available on the Centers for Disease Control and Prevention (CDC) website (cdc.gov/violenceprevention/).

Over the course of four years, the administration team was relying less on taking action after students engaged in a violent crime. Students were far less likely to experience detention or being sent out of the classroom even if they misbehaved. It was only in the rarest of instances that students experienced a consequence that separated them from instruction.

"If we want kids to learn," said Principal Gonzalez, "why are we preventing them from being in school? The research shows that students with the highest absenteeism are the ones who get in the most trouble. We're supposed to prevent that, not contribute to it."

Not everyone felt that way, however. Teacher were concerned that the rise of bullying and electronic aggression meant that the principal's methods were no longer working, and they wanted him to do something about the situation.

Issue

Principal Luis Gonzalez had turned around Metro High School, which was once considered one of the most unsafe high schools in the nation. He implemented precautionary devices and systems. He also worked with his administration team to prevent incidents from happening in the first place.

When students still found ways to misbehave, the campus didn't suspend them from class. Students were not given any excuses to miss school.

Now that bullying and electronic aggression are on the rise, the teachers are concerned that the principal's disciplinary consequences aren't as effective as they once were.

Dilemma

The teachers at Metro High School want to take disciplinary measures against students who are caught cyberbullying. Electronic aggression and bullying incidents have been steadily increasing over the past several years, even though other violent acts are decreasing.

The principal is opposed to suspending students, but it looks as though he will have to come up with a way to stop students from engaging in this behavior.

Questions for Discussion

1. How well does the principal's philosophy about suspending students from school align with current educational trends?
2. What are some of the ways a campus can give students consequences without suspending them from school?
3. What responsibility do the teachers have for preventing electronic aggression in the classroom? What about bullying?
4. How can the campus reduce and/or eliminate bullying?
5. What other violent incidents should the campus be aware of?

CASE STUDY: *BASEBALL PLAYERS ON SOCIAL MEDIA*
SUBURBAN HIGH SCHOOL
EQUITY AND CULTURAL RESPONSIVENESS, 3
COMMUNITY OF CARE AND SUPPORT FOR STUDENTS, 5

Background

Oakland High School is in an affluent suburban area where the median household income is $90,000. The high school is 92 percent white, 2 percent African American, and 5 percent Asian American. Shortly prior to and during the entire baseball season, the boys on the team exchanged racist, sexist, and homophobic remarks. During the baseball games and in the locker rooms, the boys were sending each other explicitly vulgar remarks about minority students at the high school and minorities in general.

The boys were bragging about their actions by the time baseball season had ended. The boys were showing off the pictures and the comments that they had made on a private Instagram feed where only the baseball players could join and belonged to throughout the school year. These braggadocios actions took place in front of teachers and administrators: during every single class, during group work, in science labs, as classes were transitioning in the hall way, in the cafeteria, and even in the library in front of other staff.

The Oakland High School baseball team is under investigation after racist messages were posted on social media. The posts began in a private Instagram message between some of the members of the baseball team and quickly were shared with the entire team. Members of the baseball team were discriminating against young African American women, gays, and other minorities. Disparaging comments made reference to black women as inferior, obnoxious, and ugly. Along these lines, female student identifying as lesbian, were referred to as such derogatory terms as "whores." Comments such as these were posted to a vast number of Instagram pictures, with contributions from the majority of the baseball team.

Finally, an African American senior, Tamika, at the high school went to the local media. The student drove up to the local television station, asked not to be exposed and showed all of the images with the captions to a news reporter. Tamika had taken screenshots of the images that were being sent to him via text. She explained that another student on the baseball team took her phone and deleted all of the messages. But Tamika had already taken screenshots of the texts and saved them in his photo albums multiple times. Tamika explained, with tears streaming down her eyes, that she feared for her life since she had a younger brother, a freshman, who would still be enrolled in the school and she did not want anything to happen to him if the school or community members found out about her "snitching" on the baseball team and the school. She explained that the entire school including faculty and administration knew what was going on and she showed evidence of videos that she had taken of an assistant principal looking at a baseball players phone during lunch and laughing and making vulgar remarks with the boy in the back of the cafeteria. Within minutes, the news reporter had called all major TV stations and notified them of the developing story. The news reporter explained that the repercussions were severe since the superintendent's grandson is on the baseball team. And the school administration and teachers had children who attended Oakland High School.

A court-authorized search revealed that the boys were all guilty of derogatory remarks. Despite having deleted the posts, individual culpability was traceable. A computer forensic scientist was hired by the district to generate recovery of the deleted files and found the evidence on almost all of the boys' iPhones.

The morning after the incident went public, the superintendent released a statement, "Administrators were made aware this morning of some inappropriate comments posted by students on social media and immediately took action to investigate the situation. Once the investigation is completed, administrators will make any necessary decisions regarding discipline. It is important to note that this does not represent the sentiment or overall character of our students. We will be using this as a teachable moment with students to help them grow and be prepared on how to handle these types of situations in the future."

Many in the school, students, teachers, and administration, viewed the posts. The community saw many of the posts as well. Several students were offended by the comments and debates that began online and in the school setting.

An interviewed student stated that many discussions were happening throughout the school day. Some debates were happening only between students while other conversations were happening within the classroom setting. Teachers monitored many of the in-class discussions.

The administration met with the baseball team and their parents. Without releasing all the specified disciplinary actions due to privacy concerns, the superintendent released another statement, "Consequences were given to the students according to the School District's Student Code of Conduct, as well as plans for restorative practice conferences to support a positive school culture moving forward."

A transgender student stated that "I just hope we can move on and come together as human beings so hopefully this doesn't happen again."

Students believed that the offence and resulting discipline were significantly downplayed in order to protect athletic scholarships and faculty jobs.

Issue

The Oakland baseball team was discriminating against African American women in a private group Instagram message. Due to screenshots being released, the conversation became public. Members of the baseball team were referring to African American women as inferior, obnoxious, and ugly. There was a picture of boxers, which included a caption stating that he can have girls for his own pleasure. Many Oakland High School students who saw and heard about the posts were deeply offended but took no action due to the fact that the perpetrators were related to school staff and district administration. Once administration became aware of the situation, the baseball team and their parents were brought in for disciplinary actions. Basically, the principal called the entire team and the parents for a meeting.

Dilemma

Despite school policies, the Oakland baseball team discriminated against African Americans and other minorities. Even though all members of the team were included, it gave the entire baseball program and the high school negative attention. The baseball team represents the athletic program, high school, and district. There racist comments were publicly displayed for millions of people to see. The school had to take swift action against the baseball team in order to show the behaviors were not accepted. The controversy caused chaos and hurt feelings in the school building and faculty unsure how to address the issue. With all of those negative comments, the school, administration, and team had to address such an adverse issue since it would affect future generations of athletes at the school.

Questions for Discussion

1. Why were Tamika's actions pivotal? How did she display moral courage? Would you have done what Tamika did? Why or why not?
2. What are the first steps to take in this discipline situation with the baseball team?
3. Describe approaches the school should take in order to prevent this situation from happening again.
4. Explain initiatives that can be implemented to curb future bullying situations.
5. How could the administration have handled it differently?
6. How are issues of racism, sexism, and ageism similar or different in the school setting?

CASE STUDY: *INCREASING TRANSGENDER NUMBERS*
RURAL CHARTER SCHOOL GRADES K–12
EQUALITY AND CULTURAL RESPONSIVENESS, 3A, E
COMMUNITY OF CARE AND SUPPORT FOR STUDENTS, 5A, B

Background

Mill Brook Charter School stands on a hill top, surrounded by cows and horses with the number of livestock in the town outnumber the human population. Mill Brook Charter School is a K–12 building in a rural area of the state with 780 students attending in total; that number is decreasing every year due to people moving out of the town to find jobs. Mill Brook Charter School prides itself on creating a welcoming environment for students and employees. Students enter the school willing and eager to learn, and teachers are able to build individual long-lasting relationships with their students. Bullying has not been an issue and students are encouraged to be themselves. Nobody blinks an eye when a student comes in with hot pink hair or with piercings all over. They just accept each other the way they are.

Perhaps this welcoming environment is one of the reasons that there has been an increase in transgender students at Mill Brook in the past four years. At first, there was one or two students who let teachers know they preferred a different name than their birth name or who requested different pronoun usage. The faculties were willing to accommodate these requests.

As more transgender students started enrolling, and now the enrollment of the school finally increasing for the first time in a decade, the school administration decided that it needed a policy in place so that transgender students felt welcome and were not ostracized because of their gender identity. They created a gender identity plan that the student, parent, and counselor implanted that included the students' preferred name, preferred pronouns, and preferred restroom.

Upon hearing of the policy, Jennifer Krushner, a parent of a tenth grader, scheduled a meeting with the school principal to express her concern. She was not comfortable with the idea of her daughter, Robyn, using the same restroom as a transgender student.

Issue

Mill Brook has worked really hard to create an inclusive environment. Mill Brook strives to have a school culture that is accepting to all students. With an increase in transgender students, the administration created a policy that allowed transgender students to self-identify and create a gender plan for the school. This plan included allowing the student to use the restroom of his/her gender identity. At least one parent has expressed concern over the new policy.

Dilemma

The school principal needs to create an environment where all students feel safe and supported. At the same time, she needs to ensure that students' rights are not being violated. When confronted regarding the new transgender policy in place, she must work with the parent to create a win-win situation.

Questions for Discussion

1. How does the school principal ensure that all students feel safe and supported in the school?
2. Should the school continue with the transgender plan or revise it based on parent recommendations?
3. Would the situation be different if the school was a traditional Department of Education school and not a charter school? What if it was a public school?
4. How can the situation be solved so that everyone feels heard?
5. How could the school principal prevent the concerns of one parent from escalating to multiple families?
6. Should the principal have requested family feedback before creating the policy?

Chapter 6

School Personnel

CASE STUDY: *A DAY WITHOUT*
SUBURBAN HIGH SCHOOL GRADES 9–12
PROFESSIONAL CAPACITY OF SCHOOL PERSONNEL, 6B, G, H

Background

As far as everyone could tell that the new year at Spencer High School was off to great start. The teachers were just coming back from winter break and they were looking forward to an exciting spring semester. So was the Principal Jeff Smith.

During the January in-service day, Principal Smith lead his faculty into important activities. In the morning, they analyzed data and identified learning goals for the upcoming semester as they got their children ready for state assessment. From what I could tell, they had just enough time finished teaching the concept and provide a review in an effort to prepare the children. For seniors, their performance on this test would determine whether or not they would graduate at the end of the year.

The data showed that they were on track and achieving their envisioned student outcomes.

In the afternoon, Mr. Smith led a workshop on respecting cultural differences and identifying and stopping bullying. At the end of the session, he encouraged his teachers to find ways to become involved in community as education leaders.

Mr. Smith had no idea how much he would regret his words.

In February, the nation experienced a new kind of boycott called A Day without Immigrants. The idea was that anyone who was an immigrant should stay home from work on a predetermined day, to show just how important he or she is being in the country. On the day without immigrants, many local restaurants were closed. Construction sites took the day off. Many other businesses who routinely hired immigrants limped along without them; in some cases, the emigrants returned to work the next day to learn that they had been fired.

The concept of the day without immigrants inspired many women felt disenfranchised with the new direction of politics in the nation. There had already been marches and protests about the new leadership. Women wondered how would the nation get along on a day without women.

Many of the female teachers at Spencer High School were especially curious about the answer to this question. Sixty-five percent of the faculty and staff at Spencer High School was female. Just exactly how would everyone get along if all the female teachers stayed home on A Day without Women?

Principal Smith was about to find out.

Algebra teacher Leesa Johnson had been calling the female teachers on the faculty at Spencer High School. She told them she was organizing a walkout for A Day without Women at their school. The teacher simply needed to call in sick for the day before or, if the request for an absence was denied, take the day off anyway. "Just stay home, don't show up for work," said Leesa Johnson.

Leesa was persuasive enough to convince almost two-thirds of the women on staff to just stay home on A Day without Women. She felt fairly certain that with enough pressure, she could convince the other women to stay home as well.

As the day drew nearer, Principal Smith got word of Leesa Johnson's plans. He called an emergency faculty meeting two days before the planned walkout. He told the teachers that he was more than a little disappointed in their behavior, especially when considering how excited everyone had been to focus on instruction when the semester started in January. He told the teachers that any absences without a doctor's note would be considered taking a personal day, which he had no intentions of approving.

"You have a teaching contract," he said, "and if you are healthy, I expect you to be here teaching, no exceptions." With that, Principal Smith walked out of the meeting.

Leesa Johnson stood up to address the teachers.

"That is exactly the kind of chauvinistic behavior we need to stop," said Leesa. "Who is in who is with me?" She looked at the teachers who did not raise their hands, and said, "You better raise your hands, too, if you know what's good for you."

Almost all of the women raised their hands this time. Some of the male teachers got up and walked out, and others chuckled and shook their heads.

Max Goodwell, a history department head, went to Mr. Smith's office to let him know Ms. Johnson was still organizing and planning the walkout.

Mr. Smith thanked the history teacher, and called his colleagues at the elementary school and the middle school to see if their teachers were planning a walkout too. The other principals had gotten word that something was afoot, and all they knew was that a teacher from the high school was organizing the walkout.

Mr. Smith suggested all three principals meet with the superintendent.

The superintendent listened to the principals as they explained the situation and their concerns, and she decided that the district could not risk needing so many substitute teachers on a single day. She canceled school for the day.

Many of the parents were outraged that the district would give in to the protesters. Not having school meant that they had to arrange childcare for while they were at work.

Leesa Johnson and the other female teachers were ecstatic. A day without women meant that they got the day off, with no penalty whatsoever.

"That's the power of having so many women in the field of teaching," said Leesa. "We have a voice and we will be heard." It was obvious that education could not survive without the women. This was a powerful lesson to teach their students, she felt.

There was already talk about a day without African Americans, and Leesa had already decided she would help to organize that walkout as well.

When the teachers returned from their day without women, a letter from the superintendent of schools was waiting in all of their mailboxes. In part, the letter read, "Because we closed schools due to the planned walkout for A Day without Women, we will count this day as a day of inclement conditions, and as such, we will make up the day in the summer as one of our bad weather days."

The women groaned at the news, and Leesa said, "She can't do this!"

Several of the male teachers in the workroom also groaned. One said, "Thanks for nothing, ladies. Looks like you ruined it for everything, and we're still a day short of teaching before the state exams. Way to go."

Leesa made a face at him and left the room.

"What we should have is a day without stupidity," Max Goodwell posted on his social media page when someone asked about A Day without Women.

His post earned a considerable amount of angry emojis form the female teachers, but the parents, overall, were highly supportive.

Issue

One teacher, Leesa Johnson, organized a walk-out of female teachers at the elementary, middle and high school level. Having witnessed a highly effective immigrant walk-out, Johnson believed the event would make a profound statement. She personally called the female teachers to strongly encourage them to stay home on that day.

When Principal Jeff Smith heard about the situation, he recognized the strain it would put on his campus first supervising and then teaching the students. He told the teachers that he would not approve request for personal days on this day.

He also contacted colleagues to see how many were facing a similar challenge and, based on these findings, brought the issue to the attention of the superintendent of schools.

Dilemma

Principal Jeff Smith was facing an enormous absenteeism rate among his teachers due to the national event, "A Day without Women." He was sure that there would not be enough substitutes to cover the classes needing them at his campus. He conferred with his colleagues at the elementary and at the middle schools to see if they too were facing a similar situation, and they were. The three principals decided that their next step would be to meet with the superintendent. When she heard the news, the superintendent decided to close schools on A Day without Women.

When classes resumed after A Day without Women, the faculty and staff found out that they would have to make up the missing day. They were unhappy about this, but some of the women became even unhappier when they discovered one of their colleagues posted on his own social media page that what they really needed was "A Day without Stupidity."

Questions for Discussion

1. How should Mr. Smith have stopped the walkout?
2. Was Mr. Smith in his right to deny the teachers a personal day?
3. What should Mr. Smith tell the teachers about any more plans of walkout days?
4. Obviously Ms. Johnson organized the walkout. What should Mr. Smith do about her involvement in the protest?
5. What steps does Mr. Smith need to take regarding Mr. Goodwell's social media page post?

CASE STUDY: *BODY SHAMING*
SUBURBAN HIGH SCHOOL GRADES 9–12
PROFESSIONAL CAPACITY OF SCHOOL PERSONNEL, 6D, G, H

Background

Sophia Malloy, the principal at Washington high school, was having lunch with her assistant principals. It was spring, and they were already looking ahead to the one time of year they hated the most, and that was prom.

"It's just not like it used to be," said Mrs. Malloy. "There was a time when everyone got dressed up and they look really nice."

Her assistant principals agreed.

"You know back in my day, we didn't show cleavage with everything hanging out, and we didn't have slits in our skirts up to our you-know-whats," said Mrs. Malloy.

She decided right then and there that if the girls are not going to respect themselves, the campus administration could do it for them.

Mrs. Malloy said, "What we need is guidelines for the prom—not just the rules we tell everyone about how to behave well at the party. We need a dress code. I want you to put together committee to come up with some rules about what ladies should and should not wear."

A couple of weeks later, the assistant principals met with their principal to show her what they had come up with. They had a twenty-page document explaining what dress styles, cuts, and fabrics were permissible.

Mrs. Malloy laughed. She didn't think many of the students would bother to read the document. They didn't even bother to reap the student code of conduct. Why would they read anything on the dress code for the prom? She sent the assistant principals back to the drawing board.

"Our kids are visual," said Mrs. Malloy. "You must give them something in pictures."

The assistant principals look at each other. This would be fun. They would get to surf the Internet, looking for examples of what to wear and what not to wear.

After another week went by, the assistant principals wanted to show Mrs. Malloy what they have come up with. They had thirty slides in a presentation. The slides specifically showed which dresses were considered tasteful and elegant, and which ones were considered unfit for the prom.

The presentation was titled, "Class or Trash?" and the object was for students to review the presentation and determine which outfits were appropriate and which were not.

In the presentation were examples of many different body styles and dresses. Prom dresses that were snug or slightly revealing were given the thumbs up if they were worn by then girls. Overweight girls wearing similar dresses were given the thumbs down. In addition, any dresses that showed tattoos or body piercings were labeled as Trash.

Dresses that did not go higher than just above the knee were labeled Class. So were dresses that did not show cleavage and did not have slits in the skirts.

The assistant principals went one step further, and they had a couple slides for makeup. Again, the pictures were put into two categories: Class or Trash. Excessive amounts of makeup, as well as false eyelashes and bright lipsticks, were labeled Trash. More natural and demure makeup was labeled Class.

Mrs. Malloy loved the presentation, and she wanted it sent to all the teachers since they could show it in the classroom. She knew that the girls were already looking for their prom dresses and she wanted them to purchase the right clothing. The principal asked that the presentation be uploaded to the school website just in case parents needed to see it as well.

The teachers showed the presentation in their classrooms that upset many of the girls.

"I'm already bought my dress," many of them said.

"Who is the principal to think that she can tell us what to wear to prom?" said others.

Stephanie Larson was more contemplative than that, and she didn't say anything for a while. She had always been a chunky girl—"big-boned," as her mother called it—and Stephanie was deeply hurt by the presentation. She had been looking forward to wearing a shoulderless gown. For months, she had been trying to get the courage together to bear her arms and shoulders. She had found a dress that covered her bosom without showing too much cleavage, but now, according to the presentation, because she was not like the other girls, she would not be allowed to show that much skin.

"This is body shaming," said Stephanie. "All because I don't look like the others, I am being ostracized and made fun of. This is so unfair."

Stephanie explained the situation to her parents, who agreed with her, and they offered to help plan an alternate prom where students could come wearing what they wanted without fear of being kicked out of the prom for a dress code violation.

Stephanie really wanted to go to the prom with her friends, but when she told them about the alternative prom, it seemed like many of them wanted an invitation to the A-Prom, as it was being called. The A-Prom was an opportunity to stand up to archaic and outdated definitions of style and elegance. She and her classmates took to social media to protest the dress code.

Issue

Mrs. Malloy, the principal at Washington High School, had determined that she and her administration team had a lot to define what constitutes style and elegance for the prom. They were tired of seeing girls in inappropriate dresses. This styles they disliked included those that showed too much skin, that were too short and revealing cleavage, and that had diehard slits in the skirts.

When Mrs. Malloy directed her assistant principals to prepare a slide presentation showing the difference between class and trash, the dresses and models showed a clear preference for thin girls over fat girls.

Under Mrs. Malloy's direction, the assistant principals developed a presentation that clearly privileged a specific body type.

Dilemma

When the presentation completed, Mrs. Malloy directed that Class or Trash be posted on the school website in hopes that parents and students would get the chance to review the presentation multiple times before making more prompt choices.

Mrs. Malloy got her wish.

Not only did the parents review the presentation, they made copies of it. They reported it to the local news media, indignant over how the school shows to discriminate against the girls who were going to prom.

Then the news story got picked up nationally, and it spread even further. Feminist groups began calling the school, asking for the principal but settling to talk to anyone who would pick up the phone. There were so many calls that the school had to put their answering service on and let all of the calls go to voice mail.

In the meantime, when this presentation got picked up on social media, it went viral, giving the principal and her school a bad reputation.

Questions for Discussion

1. What was the better way to handle the dress code issue?
2. What would a better title have been for the presentation?
3. Does the principal have the right to establish a dress code for the prom?
4. How could a dress code be set so that it does not discriminate against any of the students who are attending?
5. What should the principal tell Larsons about the A-prom?
6. Does the principal owe the student body apology? If so how should she go about it?

CASE STUDY: *PARENT ANARCHY*
SUBURBAN MIDDLE SCHOOL GRADES 6–8
PROFESSIONAL CAPACITY OF SCHOOL PERSONNEL, 6A
PROFESSIONAL COMMUNITY FOR TEACHERS AND STAFF, 7B
MEANINGFUL ENGAGEMENT OF FAMILIES
AND COMMUNITY, 8E

Background

Val Stevens was the principal at Rockford Middle School, which is located in a suburban area. The school has managed to maintain good reviews from the community and even better ratings from the state based on years of excellent standardized testing results.

Principal Stevens and her teachers worked hard at finding the right balance between instructions, involvement, and homework. They recognized that middle school students tend to be more socially engaged and less inclined to complete homework. To address the unique needs of the middle schooler, the faculty and staff tried to design engaging experiences for student homework.

Homework was supposed to take the average student more than ninety minutes each evening, and many of the assignments can be done through collaboration with other students. Each core subject had a designated day of the week for assigning homework, and no homework was assigned Friday through Sunday.

Regardless of the design of the homework, it was meant to be a reinforcement of the day's instruction, and it never required the students to learn something new on his or her own.

Mr. Justin is an ELA teacher at Rockford Middle School. He took his teaching seriously, and he expected his students to take his class just too seriously. Mr. Justin worked hard to prepare lessons that would help students learn and remember the skills they needed, even though Principal Stevens thought that Mr. Justin went a little overboard on planning. He was the teacher, however, who planned out the entire six weeks at one time, and he knew exactly where students should be by the end of the grading period. He planned homework assignments just as meticulously.

He expected the homework assignments to be completed—by his students, not their parents.

Several times he had parents who wrote their children's essays. Because the essays were typed on the computer, the parents thought he would not notice the syntax, word choice, and grammar that the parents used. On a couple of occasions, Mr. Justin called parents to ask them to please let their children do their homework.

Mr. Justin also talked to Principal Stevens about the matter, asking for her support and requiring students, not parents, to do the work. Mrs. Stevens mumbled something about supporting the request, and then went on about her way, forgetting to follow up. After all, how bad could it really be if parents are getting in on the homework game? At least they were participating in their child's education and knew a little bit about what was going on in the classroom. It couldn't be all bad, thought Mrs. Stevens.

Mrs. Cantu and some of the other parents thought differently. They asked to have a meeting with the principal, and they wanted to talk about Mr. Justin's teaching and his homework assignments.

Mrs. Stevens welcomed to the parents into her principal's office for the meeting. The parents let forth litany complaints about Mr. Justin. These complaints included the following:

1. The class was too hard for the average student
2. Mr. Justin expected too much from his students

3. The homework often took three hours to complete
4. Mr. Justin graded unfairly and did not even offer a curve in the classroom
5. Mr. Justin refused to let parents help their children do the homework

The principal listened to the complaints from the parents and sided with them, stating that it was not reasonable to have such unjust expectations, instruction, and homework. She certainly would talk with Mr. Justin and get him to change his ways in the classroom. The parents were pleased that the principal took their side and would do something about Mr. Justin.

Mrs. Stevens did not talk to Mr. Justin right away. Instead, several of the students in his classroom mentioned that their parents came to school to get Mr. Justin fired because he was not a good teacher.

"You still have to do the homework," said Mr. Justin. This is no excuse for getting out of an assignment. He refused to back down and continue to assign students the same amount of homework as always.

"My mom said I don't have to do your stupid homework. She's going to see to it you get fired," said one of the students.

"Well, I guess we'll just take this up with Principal Stevens," said Mr. Justin.

"Oh, my mom already has," said another student. "And you want to hear what they're saying about you on social media. That will make you think twice about being such a bad teacher."

Mr. Justin let it go for the moment and made a note to check the school's social media page during his conference period. Not too long after reading the feed, he knocked on Principal Stevens's door.

"Have you seen what the parents are saying about me?" he asked. "They are making some very ugly remarks about my teaching and the assignments that I give their children. Several of the parents I posted something about me being unfit to teach and that my license should be revoked. Did you know anything about this?"

"Um, sure, about the parent concerns," said Principal Stevens. The parents came in a while back, and they said that they were upset about the amount of homework they were assigning their children. "You know we agreed homework should only last for ninety minutes. It shouldn't take three hours to complete."

"It doesn't," said Mr. Stevens. "The kids are dragging it out, making it a bigger deal than it has to be. And now it seems like your parents are doing the same thing."

The principal told Mr. Justin that the purpose of the school was to make sure that the parents feel as though their children were getting the best education possible. If that meant bending to the parents' wishes, then so be it.

"I think you could give just a little," the principal told Mr. Justin. "after all, it is the taxpayers to pay our salaries. They need to know that they are getting value from their child's education. And if that means they need to have a say in the homework, I'm okay with that. I'm also okay with you being a little bit more flexible in the classroom. That's what our parents want."

Mr. Justin explained that he didn't feel as though he could make any revisions to his instructions or his homework assignments.

"My job is to get these kids ready for the next grade," Mr. Justin said.

"Your job is to do what the parents want," said Mrs. Stevens.

Issue

Mr. Justin is an ELA teacher at a suburban middle school where parents have become increasingly demanding. When Mr. Justin sends homework with the students on the single night set aside for completing homework in ELA, the parents complained bitterly that Mr. Justin has once again overloaded their children with unnecessary and time-consuming assignments.

Mr. Justin has repeatedly requested that the parents not do homework for their children. Instead the students may collaborate with each other in getting their work done.

The parents are up in arms about the situation and they want Mr. Justin to either change his ways or find another school in which to teach. They expect the principal to back them up and their requests.

Dilemma

When Mr. Justin spoke to Principal Stevens about parents undermining his instructional decisions in the classroom, the principal promised to take a look at every decision. She forgot to follow up. During that short interim, the parents gathered and formed a coalition to go talk to the principal about Mr. Justin.

The parents were highly vocal in expressing their dissatisfaction, and they made it very clear that they did not like Mr. Justin's teaching practices.

Not only did the parents mention this to their children, now the students refused to do class work as well as homework, and the parents also began making ugly remarks in social media about the middle school teacher.

Mr. Justin has walked into the principal's office asking a second time for her support, but she has already given it to the parents.

Questions for Discussion

1. Can a principal change her or his mind about a decision once it has been made?
2. What are the biggest mistakes Principal Stevens made?
3. What should Principal Stevens have told the parents about Mr. Justin?

4. Why is it important for principals to support their teachers in front of the parents?
5. If you were the principal, would you have sided with the parents or with the teacher in this case? Provide details that support your decision.

CASE STUDY: *MAKING THE ROUNDS*
SUBURBAN HIGH SCHOOL GRADES 9–12
PROFESSIONAL CAPACITY OF SCHOOL PERSONNEL, 6E
PROFESSIONAL COMMUNITY FOR TEACHERS
AND STAFF, 7F

Background

Mrs. Lucy Garcia is the principal at Hamilton High School, a medium-sized high school in the suburbs. Mrs. Garcia likes to make sure that her teachers have the best professional development available to them.

Each year she sends her teachers to various training, development opportunities, and conferences so that they can bring back the most promising strategies in instructional delivery and behavior management. She encourages her teachers to take reasonable risks in the classroom and apply the new things that they have learned as quickly as possible.

"The sooner you practice what you have seen, the more likely it will become a habit that we can all learn from," Mrs. Garcia liked to say to the faculty.

This year—in addition to the standard training sessions teachers were made to attend—Mrs. Garcia would implement a strenuous form of instructional rounds strongly resembling medical rounds practiced by doctors.

The principal planned to hire the substitutes necessary so that teachers could observe their colleagues in action, both in the same subject area and outside their subject area, in hopes that they would observe techniques that they could adopt and adapt to their own classrooms.

Every teacher on campus was asked to identify two teachers in their own department that they would like to observe, and two more teachers outside their department. Every teacher would get two full days of observation time. The plan was for the teachers to conference with and visit their four identified teachers in a single day conference about what happened in the classroom, and visit a second time later in the semester. At the second conference, the teacher who had been visited was inquired about the strategies implemented and how effective they were.

This would be an ongoing process throughout the first semester of school.

Overall, the teachers were very excited about the opportunity to visit their colleagues and peers. They knew that there was something teaching going on, but it was hard to see from within the confines of their own for walls.

Most of the observations went very smoothly, and several of the teachers stopped by the principal's office to thank her for this opportunity.

A couple of the teachers came by wearing concerned looks on their faces.

"Can we talk to you in private?" one of them asked. "It's about the observation."

The principal ushered the two teachers into her office. "Did something not work out right?" asked Mrs. Garcia.

The teachers looked at each other. "You can say that."

The second teacher spoke up. "It's about the math teacher Mrs. Jones. She came into both of our classrooms, and the minute she got there, she started making comments how about everything. She talked about how badly the room was arranged, she had discussions with some of the students about her assignments not what we were teaching, and she was on her phone the rest of the time. It was an uncomfortable experience, and I'm not sure that either of us are going to learn anything from it other than what not to do."

The principal promised that she would talk to Mrs. Jones about the incident and see how the experience could be improved. Mrs. Jones was, after all, a very competent teacher. Surely it was all a misunderstanding.

The first teacher had more to say.

"It's not just that. Sure, she was more disruptive than a ninth grader with raging hormones and ADHD, but it's what she did afterword that has so many of us worried. You see, while she was in the classroom, she posted pictures and video of what we were teaching our students. I didn't even know she was going to do that. And then the worst of it is that the students began using their cell phones in the classroom to make comments on what Mrs. Jones had posted. She even continued to make comments after school. I wish I was making this up, but you can see it all at the social media page."

Mrs. Garcia scheduled a meeting with Mrs. Jones.

"I understand but you have been posting inappropriate remarks how about some of the teachers on the social media pages. Their students make comments about these posts and you continued to post more comments how about your experiences making rounds on the campus. Can you explain what you were doing?"

Mrs. Jones told the principal that she had wanted to get the students involved in critiquing their classroom teacher. "It's just my little way at making sure their better teachers."

Mrs. Garcia explained that Mrs. Jones's behavior was unacceptable. It was also a violation of the acceptable use policy on the campus. Teachers are not allowed to post disrespectful comments on social networking sites.

"Well, I'm not the only one who has done it," said Mrs. Jones. If you think you have something to say to me, you better be sure you say it to everybody else who has said something snarky on social media sites how about one of the teachers or about you."

Mrs. Garcia assured Mrs. Jones that she would do exactly that.

When Mrs. Jones left the principal's office, several of her friends were concerned that they were going to get into trouble for posting unpleasant comments about their colleagues on social networking sites.

"It's okay," said Mrs. Jones. "We have rights and we are protected by the First Amendment. Ain't nobody gonna to tell me what I can cannot say!"

Issue

The high school teachers have been involved in a few professional development opportunities this year. Campus administrators made it possible for teachers to observe each other in their classrooms. The idea was that the teachers could see other experts in action as they dealt with some of the same challenges with the students at the school.

Many of the teachers appreciate the opportunity to grow professionally and be the part of community of professionals who could trust each other and provide sound advice regarding instruction and behavior management.

Not all of the teachers, however, saw this as an opportunity. Some saw this as an excuse to get out of the classroom and criticize their peers. Not only did they have a negative mindset about the experience but also the critical teachers also posted many of their thoughts in social media.

The remarks included nasty comments about the school administration and about the teachers they were supposed to visit.

Dilemma

Several of the teachers came to the campus principal, Mrs. Lucy Garcia, with concerns that their character and credibility had been damaged by the comments made by other teachers on campus. Not only were the comments made publicly on social media but also colleagues and community members alike saw the comments. The teachers felt humiliated, and all of them, when interviewed individually, pointed to Mrs. Jones as the instigator who destroyed the opportunity they could benefit from professional rounds in the classroom.

Mrs. Jones believed that teachers are protected by the First Amendment. She also convinced several of the other faculty members that day to share the same benefits and post anything they want on social media.

Mrs. Jones also went to Mrs. Garcia to ask that the principal respect her First Amendment privileges in saying whatever she would like to say.

Questions for Discussion

1. How true is it that Mrs. Jones has First Amendment rights when posting outside of the school day on other teacher social media accounts?
2. Would it have made a difference if Mrs. Jones had posted her comments outside the school day on her own time?

3. What disciplinary action should the principal take in regard to teachers making inappropriate comments made on social networking sites? Why is it important to follow through with these actions?
4. What disciplinary action can a teacher who makes inappropriate social media comments and posts be subject to? Why should a principal know this before running across it in daily campus operations?
5. How would clear and definitive parameters help the teachers have a better experience during the instructional rounds? Should principals have to remind teachers about their professional behavior? Why or why not?
6. Should principals who are hiring new teachers request to see a candidate's social media page? Why or why not?

Chapter 7

Professional Staff

CASE STUDY: *BULLIES AND DEMONS*
SUBURBAN HIGH SCHOOL GRADES 9–12
PROFESSIONAL COMMUNITY FOR TEACHERS
AND STAFF, 7C, G

Background

Julia Beach wanted one thing for her son more than anything else. She wanted him to have a normal education. At least, as normal as it could be.

John Beach had been in special education since he was in the first grade. He tried very hard to make sense of what the teachers are signing class, but it was very difficult and it wore him out. Special education gave John access to both the curriculum and sense of success shared by his peers.

John's mom worked with the school and the teachers in middle school to make sure that John felt safe when he was in class and that the middle school-ers did not torment him. When John went to high school, Mrs. Beach met with the principal of the school.

"Mr. Hancock," she said, "I know you have many students to care about, but I want you to understand that John is the only child I have to care about. I am placing him in your hands for his care and safety, and for him to enjoy his high school experience."

Mr. Hancock told Mrs. Beach not to worry. John would be as safe at Miller High School as he would be anywhere. No harm would come to her son.

Secretly, Principal Hancock didn't care about the whole special education business and thought it was a ridiculous waste of money, and that kids who needed to be in special education ought to be institutionalized. You never share the sentiments with anyone at the school, but we talked about these feelings at home in front of his wife and his son, who was also a ninth grader at the same school.

John Beach was on his way to his favorite class, music appreciation. He was running late because he had been delayed in the restroom. Now he was in a hurry to get to music appreciation because he did not want to interrupt the teacher once class started. He also did not want to miss any of the music they were studying.

"Must hurry, must hurry, must hurry," he said under his breath to no one but himself. John was so focused about getting himself to the music class that he didn't notice a group of boys hanging out by the lockers at the end of the hallway. John had to walk past them to get to the music room.

"Hey you big goon," said one of the boys. "What a dummy, talking to yourself in the hallway, just like a broken record," he said. "You oughtta be in an institution. My dad even says so."

"Yeah," said another one of the boys. "And do you know what they'll do to you when you get there? They are going to tie you up like this, and they'll beat you too."

The boys grabbing John's arms and pinned him against the lockers. They took thin rope they had found and lashed John's wrists against the holes in the locker handles along the top row, and then they tied his feet to the locker handles along the bottom row.

The bullies took turns punching John in the gut. He cried out and wailed against his assailants. "Please, please stop hitting me. I didn't do anything to you. Please stop. I just want to go to music class."

The beating continued.

"Please let me go and I won't say anything. Not to anyone. I promise."

In the shadows of the end of the hallway, a figure paused for a moment as if taking in the situation at the lockers, and then it continued on its way without saying anything.

When John couldn't take it anymore, the lead bully said, "What a sissy. You're such a little baby, you're not even worth beating up." He reached out with a knife.

John shut his eyes as tightly as he could. The bully cut the rope tying John's wrists to the lockers.

"Did you get that?" the bully asked. One of the other bullies had been videotaping the beating.

"Yeah, it was pretty funny. We gotta post this and see what people say!"

"Dude, this is going to be so cool!"

The boys fled from the scene, leaving John to figure out how to free his ankles. It looked like he was going to miss all of music appreciation. All he wanted to do was go home.

The bullies posted their video online, and it went viral in no time. Many people were aghast at what they saw, but others cheered for the bullies. Within a matter of hours, the video had been seen by a large number of people.

One of them called Mrs. Beach. She watched the video in horror, finally understanding why her son had been so upset when he came home from school.

The next day Mrs. Beach furiously stormed into the principal's office.

"Is this your idea of safety, Mr. Hancock?" She thrust her phone at the principal. The video of John was playing on it.

Mr. Hancock had already seen the video because his son had showed it to him the night before.

"What do you want me to do about this?" said Mr. Hancock. "Obviously your son did something to offend these boys, and they were just taking matters into their own hands. That's what boys do."

"You promised my son would be safe," said Mrs. Beach. "He was not safe. He was beaten up. I know the school has cameras, and I want to see the video of my son on the school's camera system. I want to see what happened before and after he got beaten up."

That was the last thing that Mr. Hancock wanted to do. Showing that video would mean that someone would figure out who was at the end of the hallway during the beating. The principal did not want anyone to know that it was him.

Issue

Special education student John Beach was on his way to music appreciation when he was detained in the hallway, tied up, and beaten by the group of boys of his age who also videotaped the incident so they could post it in social media later.

One of the boys was the principal's son, who stated that his father believed that special education students should be institutionalized, and that his dad was right. The boys left John in the hallway afterward.

Mrs. Beach wants to know from the principal why her son was not protected. She has demanded to see the video from the school's cameras so that she could see what happened before and after the incident.

Dilemma

The principal, Mr. Hancock, was at home when he mentioned to his son, who is also a freshman at the school, that special education students ought to be institutionalized. The son, who was a known bully at the school, gathered some of his friends, and they cornered John Beach to beat him up. They made a video of their efforts.

Mr. Hancock saw the beating take place. He was the figure at the end of the hall who paused to watch the beating happen before heading to another location.

Now Mrs. Beach wanted to see that footage, and he couldn't possibly let her do it because then she would know that he did nothing to stop her son's assailants.

Questions for Discussion

1. What should Mr. Hancock do about the video that his son posted?
2. What should Mr. Hancock do about the video that the school's cameras captured?
3. Does Mr. Hancock have a right to express his personal beliefs about education outside the school environment?
4. What consequences should the bully face?
5. What consequences do you think Mr. Hancock should face?
6. What support Will John Beach need at school?

CASE STUDY: *SUGAR AND SPICE*
SUBURBAN HIGH SCHOOL GRADES 9–12
PROFESSIONAL COMMUNITY FOR TEACHERS AND STAFF, 7D
ETHICS AND PROFESSIONAL NORMS, 2A
COMMUNITY OF CARE AND SUPPORT FOR STUDENTS, 5D

Background

Marvin Fox taught science at Carter High School. This high school was a medium-sized campus in the suburbs, and Mr. Fox was well liked by students, the faculty, and parents. Mr. Fox has not had any behavior issues, and his teaching was good. He himself had never been reprimanded for anything.

He seemed like the kind of nice guy who always wanted to help others out. He often stayed late to tutor students, and he even allowed students to repeat some of the lab work that they didn't understand during class. Mr. Fox also permitted some of his students to be his lab "assistants."

Mr. Fox frequently wrote passes requesting that students, male and female alike, be permitted to come to science if they weren't busy in their other classes. He needed the assistance, he said, and besides, the extra work in science never hurts anybody.

Mr. Fox's favorite student assistant was Jessica White. Even at fifteen, she reminded Marvin of his former wife, who had died during childbirth shortly after they were married. His wife delivered a baby girl, but she too, died early, in her teens. Now Mr. Fox was single, and he devoted all of his time to his students at school.

He especially seemed to like spending time with Jessica White, and she liked the attention she was receiving from an older man.

Jessica's English teacher, Mrs. Masters, often let Jessica leave English to go to the science room if she was finished with her work. How surprised Mrs. Masters would have been to learn that Jessica was visiting Mr. Fox during his conference period.

The real challenge came when one of the cheerleaders happened to be walking past Mr. Fox's classroom. She glanced through the window in the door, and something caught her eye, so she paused to see what was going on.

She could just barely see two people in the farthest corner of the classroom, and they were in an embrace, kissing each other. As her eyes focused on the couple, the cheerleader could tell that the man was Mr. Fox, the science teacher. Her eyes widened with surprise when she recognized who he was kissing. Mr. Fox was kissing her tenth grade classmate Jessica White.

The cheerleader raised her cell phone and snapped a quick photo. Then she posted it on a picture sharing social media site. The caption beneath the photo said, "Guess who?"

As soon as she posted the photo, the game was on. Many of the students at the high school participated in the guessing game. Most of them recognized right away that the teacher was Mr. Fox, that single, older science teacher who loved his work more than anything else. Until today that is. Apparently, there is someone else he was fond of as well: one of their classmates, Jessica White.

When the principal, Eddie Strauss, found out what was going on, he immediately asked Mr. Fox to come to his office, where he reprimanded the teacher and said this sort of behavior is not allowed.

The principal promised to document the incident in writing and place a letter in the teacher's file.

What the principal did not realize is that the English teacher Mrs. Masters continued to let Jessica leave her English classroom to visit Mr. Fox during his conference period. Mrs. Masters had no interest in social media, and was not aware of all of the digital gossip going on at the school. Mrs. Masters always avoided the teachers' lounge and ate lunch alone on the classroom.

A second student happened to see Mr. Fox and Jessica and in another embrace in his classroom, and she too reported it to the principal. Mr. Strauss called Mr. Fox into his office again, and once again he reprimanded the teacher, saying that he was going to place a separate letter in his file. If the teacher was caught the third time, the principal felt compelled to take the matter higher.

Mr. Fox said he understood.

The principal realized that he had forgotten to write the first letter of reprimand, and now he had a second one to write. Rather than write two separate letters, and backdate one of them, the principal decided to documents in both incidents in one letter for the sake of expediency.

On Thursday, Mr. Fox did not report to work. He had called in for a substitute teacher to handle his classes for Thursday and Friday. It seemed that he had every intention of returning to work on Monday after a four-day weekend because he did not request a substitute for the following week. When Monday rolled around, Mr. Fox did not show up for work.

Principal Strauss was concerned that something might have befallen the teacher over the weekend. He was shocked to learn how close he was to guessing that something indeed had happened.

Jessica White's parents came to school the same Monday morning that Mr. Fox was absent, wanting to know if anyone at the school had seen their daughter Thursday, Friday, or Monday. They had not seen their daughter since they said goodbye to her Thursday morning just before she left for school.

Mr. Strauss was starting to get a nauseated feeling in his stomach. He asked the parents to sit down, and he explained to them that one of the teachers, Mr. Marvin Fox, had been seen kissing Jessica not once, but twice on the campus.

In addition, Mr. Fox had also been absent since Thursday and had not returned to work. Perhaps there was a connection?

The principal assured the parents that he had reprimanded the teacher. In doing so, he had thought the issue was resolved.

Clearly he was mistaken.

Issue

One teacher at the high school campus is a likely pedophile. He exhibits many of the classic characteristics of red flag behavior such as being good with kids and being well liked and trusted by other adults, and manages to get students alone with no other adult supervision. The other teachers are unwittingly allowing his behavior to continue by permitting students from their classrooms to visit the teacher in question.

The teacher, Mr. Fox, has been seen twice by other students as he was kissing another one of his students during his conference period. Both times, the witnesses reported to the school principal what they saw.

Principal Strauss reprimanded Mr. Fox both times, but now Mr. Fox has abandoned his job and very likely taken the student with him.

The police issued an Amber Alert for Jessica.

Dilemma

Science teacher Mr. Fox was not removed from his position at the high school. Instead he was allowed to continue working in close contact with students while still in the role of classroom teacher. He was permitted unsupervised contact with students.

Mr. Strauss also failed to properly document the incident in which Mr. Fox was seen kissing a fifteen-year-old student, and he did not have the teacher removed from the classroom.

When the same incident happened the second time, the principal still did not have the teacher removed, and he merely told the teacher to stop it, and that he would document the incident in a written letter that stayed in the teacher's personnel file on the campus.

The teacher was absent for two days before the weekend, and was absent again on Monday. The student he had been kissing—Jessica White—was also absent the same days as her teacher. Mr. Strauss did not contact the parents after either incident, and he did not call child protective services, either.

The parents and the authorities fear that Mr. Fox has kidnapped Jessica, who is a minor student. Mr. and Mrs. White are sitting in Mr. Strauss's office, and they are furious with his lack of action and inept handling of the situation. They are sure that their daughter's absence could have been prevented if the principal has taken a more active role.

Mr. Strauss is now worried about more than just Mr. Fox and Jessica; he is worried about his job.

Questions for Discussion

1. What's wrong with the way Mr. Strauss documented the first incident of kissing between the teacher and the student?
2. What should Mr. Strauss have done when the kissing incident was reported the second time?
3. Why is the teachers' habit of letting students go to other classes during their instructional a problem? How should this problem be addressed on the campus?
4. Can Mr. Strauss be considered an accomplice? Why or why not?
5. How true is it that Mr. Strauss's job is on the line? Should he be worried? Why or why not?

CASE STUDY: *ARRESTED PRINCIPAL*
URBAN HIGH SCHOOL GRADES 9–12
PROFESSIONAL COMMUNITY FOR TEACHERS AND STAFF, 7C, E
COMMUNITY OF CARE AND SUPPORT FOR STUDENTS, 5E

Background

Principal Brandy Jacobs was the lead administrator in one of the roughest urban high schools in the city. This school had already been named an inner city unsafe school. That meant that's the school had far too many violent episodes in the past. If the pattern of violent behavior on the campus continued, the school would have to close, and everybody working at the school may or may not have a job at another school district.

Mrs. Jacobs and her faculty recognized that tough neighborhoods surrounded the campus. The neighborhood regularly saw gang action. Members loitered on the streets, sold drugs, and fought with each other. Some people never went back home again.

The school was far safer than the neighborhood itself.

It was standard practice to have three or four fights on her campus every. Most of the fights were small altercations, usually pushing and shoving, but occasionally, there were some knock down drag out fights that involved bodily injury. The girls fought just as often as the boys.

Principal Jacobs and her assistant principals had received training in how to properly restrain students so they could keep them from hurting each other, but none of the administrators wanted to step in the middle of the serious fight, especially if it was a girls' fight.

They agreed that girl fights were far more dangerous than any fights involving the boys, and trying to separate fighting girls ensured that they would be injured as well.

So far none of the fights at the high school had involved a gun, and for that, Principal Jacobs and her assistant principals were thankful. If they didn't want to get in the middle of a fist fight, they certainly didn't want to be in the middle of gunfire. They also didn't want the other high school students to be in such a dangerous situation.

It would be practically impossible to provide safety for students if there was a gun on campus.

On a Monday morning, classes were about to start, Principal Jacobs was told there was a fight in the cafeteria. Two groups of girls had become angry with each other. This started name calling and getting up in each other's faces. Then somebody pushed another person, and somebody else pulled the girls' hair, and the fight was on.

Mrs. Jacobs wished that she hadn't chosen to wear heels that morning, but she ran to the fight anyway. On her way there, she overheard one of the students saying, "There's a gun in the cafeteria." The principal took in this information, and she ran faster. At the same time, she pulled out her cell phone and dialed 911.

She gave the operator the school address, and said that there was a gun on the campus and there was a fight under way. She requested help from the police department.

When the police arrived in the cafeteria, Mrs. Jacobs was already trying to get the girls to break apart from each other and calm down. The assistant principals had cleared the cafeteria, and only the fighting girls were left.

Mrs. Jacob was hollering at the girls. Her words were like water thrown on a hornet's nest. They seem to make the girls even madder.

One of the police officers blew his whistle, making a loud shrill sound. It got the girls' attention.

Every one of the students who were fighting was handcuffed and taken to a squad car. They were being arrested for disturbing the peace and creating a potentially volatile situation. The police officers demanded to know where the gun was. They interviewed each girl individually, and every one of them said, "There is no gun."

The officers tried to explain that there had to be a gun because that's why they were called out to the school. They certainly would not have come had it been just a fight.

Then the officers turned to the principal. "Mrs. Jacobs," they asked, "where is the gun you told the 911 operator about?"

"How should I know?" exclaimed Mrs. Jacobs. "I just got here to break up the fight, like you. You didn't find a gun?"

"Are you trying to joke with us Mrs. Principal?" asked another officer on the scene. "Because it ain't funny. Either there is a gun, or there's not a gun. For your sake, you better hope that there is a gun."

Mrs. Jacobs put her hands on her hips. "It sounds like you are trying to threaten me. Is that your intent, sir?"

"Do you feel threatened?" asked the officer. "Because if there is no gun, you are going to be in a lot of trouble. It's called filing a false report, and you can be arrested for that. Pay a fine. Even go to jail."

"What are you talking about," asked Mrs. Jacobs. "I have not seen a gun. I was told by another student that there was a gun in the cafeteria. I called you to help me handle this situation."

"Who was the student?" asked an officer.

"I don't know," said Mrs. Jacobs. "I was running, trying to get to the cafeteria before someone got seriously hurt. It was all a blur."

When the girls were taken to station for processing, Mrs. Jacobs had the assistant principals contact their parents.

When it seems as though chaos of the morning had finally calmed, and Jacobs could finally take a deep breath, two of the police officers returned. They stopped the principal in the hallway.

"Mrs. Jacobs, you are under arrest for filing a false report with the city Police Department. Please come with us."

A warning for the first time, the second time you'll get a fine, keep it up and you get to have some jail time.

Issue

Mrs. Jacobs is the principal at an urban high school known for its violence. The school already has an unsafe designation, and is trying to turn that around.

However, the neighborhoods surrounding the school are particularly violent, and the school is actually the safest place for students. In spite of that, there are often fights that break out on the campus, but most of them do not result in physical injury. In fact, there has not even been a gun on the campus so far.

When girls' fight broke out in the cafeteria, Mrs. Jacobs went to stop the fight. On the way to the cafeteria, she overheard another student remark that there was a gun in the cafeteria. The principal dialed 911. When the police officers arrived at the school, they helped to break up the fight, handcuffed the girls, and took them back to the station for booking. They never found a gun.

Dilemma

Mrs. Jacobs has been charged with a felony offense. Specifically, she has been charged with disorderly conduct and making a false police report, all because she called the police to report that there was a gun on campus, when in fact there was no gun at all.

She was humiliated by being arrested in the halls of her school, and the community was furious that although the principal acted in a way that she could best ensure the safety of all students, she had been arrested.

District policy required that anyone under suspicion of a felony be removed from the campus pending an investigation.

Mrs. Jacobs had every intention of using her time away from her duties to retain an attorney so that she could sue the city police department.

Questions for Discussion

1. Did Mrs. Jacobs do the right thing by calling 911 when she thought there was a gun on campus? Should she have confirmed its presence first? Why or why not?
2. How would your answer be different if she placed the call just so she didn't have to separate the fight herself?
3. Can Mrs. Jacobs use her leave time to work with an attorney? Why or why not?
4. Does the school principal have the right to sue the police department? Should she be worried about the district's position on the matter?
5. How can the administrative team at the high school reduce the number of fights that are happening? Make recommendations that could help them overturn their unsafe school status.

Chapter 8

School and Community Relations

CASE STUDY: *SOCIAL MEDIA SLURS*
SUBURBAN MIDDLE SCHOOL GRADES 6–8
MEANINGFUL ENGAGEMENT OF FAMILIES
AND COMMUNITY, 8F, I
COMMUNITY OF CARE AND SUPPORT FOR STUDENTS, 5A

Background

Luke Ender was a seventh grade student at Middlebrook Middle School. He suffered from hypertrichosis cubiti, a condition in which excessive amounts of hair grows on the skin around the elbows. The hair is often long and silky.

Luke hated the hair that grew from his elbows because he thought it made him look weird. He did everything he could to hide his elbows. He wore long-sleeved shirts, even when the weather was warm. Everyone else would be outside playing and wearing short sleeves, and Luke would try to keep up panting and sweating in the heat of the sun while wearing long sleeves. In addition, he had tiny hands and a small mouth that arched upward. He was a small kid, short of stature.

And for all of these reasons, the kids in school called him Monkey Boy. He was teased in elementary school, but for the most part, the teasing subsided when he began wearing long-sleeved shirts every single day.

In middle school, however, students dressed for PE, and they had to wear a uniform. In the warmer months, the uniform consisted of a short-sleeved shirt. That meant that everyone could see Luke's elbows.

"Monkey Boy, Monkey Boy," they cried.

"Hey, what are you, some kind of weird werewolf?" asked another student.

And that was mild compared to what they wrote in social media posts about Luke.

For all of these reasons, Luke hated school.

Luke's mom made an appointment with the coach. She wanted to talk to the coach to see if there wasn't something that could be done for Luke. She hated that he had to wear short sleeves just because it was part of the uniform.

The coach listened to Luke's mom's concerns, and then he told the parent that rules were rules, and everybody, including Luke, had to follow them. Besides, a little teasing wouldn't hurt him. It might even make him stronger and more confident. One day he was going to have to learn how to stand up for himself, and learning how to deal with his condition in middle school just might help him do that.

Luke's mom was unhappy with the outcome of the conversation. She made an appointment with the principal.

The principal, Lee Shannon, had already met Luke.

"I hear that Luke is a great kid," said Mr. Shannon. "According to his teachers, he is a quick learner, but he is quiet and shy in the classroom."

Luke's mom explained about the medical condition that plagued her son.

"That explains a lot," said Mr. Shannon. "I had also heard Luke had difficulty getting along with his peers in the classroom. He does not always make friends easily."

"Can you blame him?" asked Luke's mom. "Most of the other children make fun of him. They call him Monkey Boy and other names. Even the girls have teased him because of his condition. I have to tell you even though he is a good student he no longer wants to come to school. I think he's going through depression."

"You should see what they write and social media about him," she continued. "It's not okay, I tell you. No child should have to suffer that kind of humiliation. Can't you do something about it?" the mom asked.

Principal Shannon said, "Yes, that can happen in middle school. It can be a difficult place to make friends. It's even hard to fit in. I remember my middle school days, and I am so glad that I do not have to repeat them. But we all go through it, and we survive. We even survive the ugly things other people say. I'm sure Luke will survive them too."

Luke's mom was shocked at what the principal said. She knew her son was having difficulty, and she expected to have more support than what she got.

By the end of the week, Luke refused to go to school at all. He didn't want to get dressed, and he did not want to get in the car. His mom called the principal for advice on what to do.

"Just put him in the car," said Mr. Shannon, "PJs and all. Bring him to school and drop him off, along with the change in regular clothes. I'm sure that by the end of first semester, he's going to want to be in jeans and shirt not his PJs."

Luke arrived at school in the backseat of his mother's car. A couple of the staff members escorted Luke to the building, where he ran immediately to a restroom and refused to come out. They left this change of clothes in the restroom for him.

During third period, one of the girls was walking by the boys' restroom. She heard sobbing coming from inside the restroom. Very cautiously, she opened the door.

"Are you okay," she said. "Do you need help?"

There were more cries.

The student stepped inside to see what the problem was. There sat Luke on floor. His clothes were scattered around him, and he was still wearing his PJs. His tear-stained face looked up at his classmate, and he said, "Please help me." When she looked closer, she could tell that a black eye was already forming, the lower lip was busted, and Luke seemed to have other bruises on his arms as well.

The girl ran to get her teacher, who called the nurse and the counselor. They went immediately to Luke's rescue.

Luke, now wearing his regular clothes, was sitting in the nurse's office when his mother arrived at school. He was holding an ice pack over his eye and sipping an orange juice.

"I want to go home, Mom," Luke said. "Can't you homeschool me or something?"

"First things first," said his mom. "Do you know who did this to you?"

Luke nodded, "But I'm not supposed to tell."

"Luke you're going to have to be very brave and tell who did this so we can put a stop to it. And then I want to go see the principal again."

Issue

Luke is a middle school student who presented with an unusual and rare condition that causes long silky hairs to grow from the skin around his elbows. Usually he covers up the hair by wearing long sleeves, but the shirts are hot in the warmer months. The middle school rules require that Luke dress out for PE and that meant wearing the appropriate PE uniform in class. Failure to do so meant that his grade would be lowered.

Instead, the coach refused to allow for an exception, and Luke didn't want to come to school anymore because of the bullying he experienced. The other students called him names and wrote similar slurs in social media about Luke and his condition.

When forced to come to school, Luke gets beat him in the boy's restroom.

Dilemma

The coach refused to listen to the student's concerns or those of the student's mother. He instead dismissed the bullying as nothing severe, calling it something everyone goes through to become stronger and more confident.

When Luke's mom met with the principal, he said something similar. He did not think the bullying was as bad as she made it out to be. He told her that he remembered getting bullied in school, and he came a better person for it, although he wouldn't want to repeat the experience.

When Luke refused to come to school, the principal suggested that the parents should force him to attend, even if it meant dropping him off in his PJs with a change of clothes.

The parents took the principal's suggestion, and Luke ran to a restroom. When he was rescued during third period, he had been beaten up.

Questions for Discussion

1. Where did Mr. Shannon fail as a principal?
2. What support services can the school provide Luke?
3. Should the girl who went into the boys' restroom have consequences for going into an all-male environment?
4. Can the students who beat up Luke be held responsible for the attack? What about their attacks in cyberspace on social media posts?
5. What can be done to accommodate Luke's special needs?

CASE STUDY: *ON HOLIDAY*
RURAL MIDDLE SCHOOL GRADES 6–8
MEANINGFUL ENGAGEMENT OF FAMILIES
AND COMMUNITY, 8A, B, C

Background

West Middle School was a small school in the country. The school did a good job providing a basic education their students. The students went to elementary, middle school, and high school in West, and often they stayed right there in town to become part of community after graduation.

Life in West was simple, and it was consistent. Little ever changed.

In recent years, though, people begin moving to West from some of the bigger cities. Eventually, the school's population became more diverse. With the diverse population came diverse cultures as well.

The district, however, still liked to do things the same way it had always done them. They even had a traditional calendar for the school year.

Each year, the students got the same holidays off. Most of these were really important days, such as Thanksgiving, Christmas, Easter, spring break, and

Memorial Day. Just recently this school has been allowed to observe Martin Luther King Day as a holiday.

Other noteworthy holidays were observed at school, rather than take a day off for them. These holidays included 9/11, Christopher Columbus Day, Veterans Day, and Presidents' Day.

All in all, it was a good calendar that had served the district and the school well for many years.

However, parents whose children attended West Middle School wanted special holidays for their families. They didn't like that some holidays were recognized but not others.

Mrs. Olsen, the principal at West Middle School, held a parent meeting at the school to listen to the parents' concerns. She printed copies of the school calendar for the past three years.

"What holidays do you want that we are not already taking?" she asked. "There are only so many available days in the school year."

One of the mothers asked to be recognized. "Why is it that we observe Christmas break, and not winter break? Not all of us celebrate Christmas. Some of the celebrate Hanukkah, and to collect Christmas is an affront."

Mrs. Olsen tried to explain that the meeting was for seeing what need there was for other holidays, not changing the names of the ones they already had.

Another parent stood up and cleared his throat. "We would like to have a holiday for the celebration off," the parent said. "For us, it is the Festival of Sacrifice, and a holy day indeed. Our other important holy day, Eid al-Fitr, occurs in the summer and is of no matter or consequence to the schools."

"I imagine it will be if we have to keep pushing days around," said Mrs. Olsen. "Who else?"

A group of families who were sitting together had been excitedly discussing their ideas. Mr. Gonzales was chosen to speak for the group. "I think we would all agree to have Cinco de Mayo as a holiday. It would be in May, or course, and it would give everyone a nice break. Of course, we can also celebrate 16 September as well," he said.

"I'm pretty sure we're not going to celebrate holidays from other countries," said Mrs. Olsen. "We don't have time to celebrate our own holidays."

The principal reminded everyone that she had promised to take their concerns to the superintendent. She wrote the list of recommended holidays on a large piece of tablet paper so that she writes down the number of votes for each holiday.

She called them out and wrote down the votes:

Eid al-Adha? 7 votes.
Yom Kippur? 3 votes.
? 23 votes.

Someone else stood up. "I have an idea," he said. "Let's count votes for keeping the holidays we already have, or, for the sake of diversity, let's celebrate a holiday from every major culture in the world. How many are in favor of celebrating the Chinese New Year?" There was laughter and he sat down.

Mrs. Olsen tried to explain that she was attempting to take their concerns seriously. However, there were so few votes for the holidays that she didn't see the reason to take the parents' concerns to the superintendent.

Instead she told the parents that she would approve any holidays parents wanted their children to take for religious purposes. If students needed to be absent for Eid al-Adha, Yom Kippur, or Cinco de mayo, they could take that day to celebrate their heritage and their culture, and that the absence would be counted as an excused absence.

"Now wait just a minute," said Mr. Muakkadah. "That's the whole problem, right there. The other students are not counted absent for their religious and cultural holidays. You are saying that my child can take the day off but will be counted absent. That is not okay. He will no longer have perfect attendance."

Mrs. Olsen tried to explain that these were the rules, and it was the best that she could do. After all, very few families in this school celebrated any of the holidays she had written on that chart paper.

"I simply do not see a need for it. Cinco de mayo isn't even a religious holiday," said Mrs. Olsen. "If you have issues, you should take them up with the superintendent."

Issue

West has always been a traditional community, and they liked it that way. The people who live there have gone to school in West made their living in West and raise their families in West. They have seen very little change in their community until recently.

The families at West Middle School feel as though their cultures are not respected or recognized because their holidays are not on the school calendar. As the school has become more diverse, they argued, so should the calendar. The days that students get to celebrate religious and cultural events must reflect the population at the school and in the community.

Mrs. Olsen, the principal, believes that it is better for students to take the days they need, and she will simply count their absences as excused absences.

Dilemma

Mrs. Olsen has alienated the parents at West Middle School several ways. First, she failed to recognize the cultural heritage of the families who make up the population at West Middle School. Second, she wrote off their holy days that they had requested for a holiday as being insignificant and trivial compared to the holidays already on the calendar. In addition, she made flippant remarks about the inconvenience that the additional holidays would cause.

By the end of the meeting, Mrs. Olsen decided that none of these requests needed to be taken up with the superintendent. If the parents wanted to talk to the superintendent they could do so on their own. She was no longer going to be their go-between. They would have to do it on their own.

Questions for Discussion

1. How could Mrs. Olsen have shown greater understanding of the parents' concerns?
2. Why is it unfair to give the students an excused absence?
3. How should Mrs. Olsen have handled the individual parent concerns?
4. What recommendations should Mrs. Olsen make to the district in preparation for the upcoming academic calendar?
5. How can Mrs. Olsen be sure that her campus addresses the changing diversity in the school?

CASE STUDY: *MOVING ON UP*
SUBURBAN HIGH SCHOOL
MEANINGFUL ENGAGEMENT OF FAMILIES AND
COMMUNITY, 8C, D

Background

Lynn Romero could read between the lines pretty well. As the principal of a large suburban high school for the past seven years, she had become perceptive about the school data she was reviewing.

The College Board had just released the recent SAT scores for Clear Stream Public Schools (see table 8.1). Principal Romero's high school, Boulder, had not performed well compared to the other high schools in the district. The SAT scores had actually increased just a little this year from past year, but she wondered if that would be enough to prevent more families from moving to other high schools.

Parents had been perceptive enough to figure out that their children would have the best chance of getting into prestigious universities if they graduated from Cliffside High School. Two years ago, there had been a mad dash to move into the Cliffside neighborhoods, and as a result, property values had skyrocketed. The campuses even had waiting lists for teachers who wanted to work there.

Getting into the right university, preferably with Ivy League classification, was everything, and that meant getting into the right public high school. Most of the parents in the area couldn't afford the $80,000 a year tuition for a private college preparatory academy, so instead, they handpicked their public

Table 8.1   SAT scores in Clear Steam Public Schools.

School	Reading	Math	Writing	Total
Rockview HS (2017) (2016)	612	625	601	1838
	599	620	595	1814
Pebblebrook HS (2017) (2016)	590	592	574	1756
	575	590	560	1725
Boulder HS (2017) (2016)	570	581	560	1711
	560	575	559	1694
Eddy HS (2017) (2016)	588	611	586	1785
	572	604	579	1785
Stone Canyon HS (2017) (2016)	584	601	571	1756
	570	602	579	1751
Cliffside HS (2017) (2016)	722	757	714	2193
	715	755	716	2186

Sample data based on the College Board website (collegeboard.org)

high schools. There were rumors that some of the homeowners in the Cliffside area had started renting out mother-in-law apartments in their homes so that the parents living in Boulder, Eddy, and Stone Canyon could have a Cliffside address for their children.

Principal Romero recognized that although her school had some of the lowest SAT scores in the district, they were still higher than those in the surrounding counties. That meant some families were opting to live in the Boulder High School neighborhoods, but the family demographics were far different than what the principal and her teachers had seen before. Perceptive parents were trying to move on up, and they knew education was the ticket to success for their children.

Many of these families were immigrants from diverse countries. Over the past three years, Principal Romero had seen quite a change in the demographics of her school. Where the school once consisted mostly of families who spoke only English, those numbers were rapidly dwindling. Now far less than half the families with children enrolled at Boulder High School spoke English as their first language. There had been a tremendous increase in Arabic-speaking families, and other ethnicities were moving into the neighborhoods surrounding the schools as well. She has always wanted more family and community involvement in her school.

For the principal and her faculty, that meant teaching for cultural diversity as well as preparing students for the rigors of college work. Teachers had to include instructional strategies for teaching English as a second language as well as teaching difficult content.

Principal Romero wanted to do much more for her students. She wanted to position Boulder High School to be a leading school in the district, one on par with Rockview and Cliffside high schools.

These two schools had been able to create a focus within their schools. Both implemented STEM programs for students, and their math scores showed it. Rockview developed a well-respected robotics and hydraulics program for students. The campus partnered with a nearby university to enhance collaboration between high school and college students. Cliffside developed an intensive microbiology program for students interested in the medical field. Both campuses had an exceptionally high number of teachers certified to teach IB/AP classes.

Principal Romero looked at the teaching certifications for her faculty. She had 23 percent fewer IB/AP certified teachers than the top-performing high schools in the district, and Boulder High School had no well-developed program of interest—no "draw" that would inspire student enrollment or exceptional teachers.

She would have to come up with a plan to move Boulder High School into a better position to increase student enrollment as well as student performance.

Issue

For the second year in a row, the SAT scores at Boulder High School have been the lowest in the school district. Two other campuses in the district have been performing particularly well, possibly because of their STEM programs, and as a result, many families are trying to move into the neighborhoods around those high schools. They are moving away from the Boulder High School neighborhoods.

The families moving into the neighborhood around Boulder High School are predominantly English as a second language speakers. Their native languages include Spanish, Arabic, Tagalog, and Russian (see table 8.2).

The Boulder High School faculty is having to change the way it delivers instruction and prepare students for greater rigor in academics.

Dilemma

The principal would like to create a rigorous program at Boulder High School that would draw families and increase student enrollment. The SAT scores

Table 8.2   Boulder High school's non-native speaking families.

	English-only-speaking families	Spanish-speaking families	Arabic-speaking families	Tagalog-speaking families	Russian-speaking families
2017	37	38	15	5	5
2016	53	35	10	1	1
2015	74	22	4	0	0

Sample data based on the College Board website (collegeboard.org)

at her high school are consistently low in reading, mathematics, and writing. Two other schools in the district already have outstanding STEM programs. They have a high number of teachers who are IB-/AP-certified.

The principal needs more IB-/AP-certified teachers on her campus, as well as a rigorous academic program, much like what a magnet school would offer. The problem is that the principal had no idea where to begin as funds are limited.

Questions for Discussion

1. Who should the principal reach out to for support and why?
2. How can the principal involve the community in revamping Boulder High School?
3. What can the principal do to involve the faculty and assessing their strengths and weaknesses?
4. How can the principal get and retain more IB-/AP-certified teachers and offer more rigorous courses for students?
5. What sort of supports should the school be prepared to provide students and their families?

Chapter 9

Facilities Management

CASE STUDY: *THE DIRTY DOZEN*
RURAL MIDDLE SCHOOL GRADES 6–8
OPERATIONS AND MANAGEMENT, 9K

Background

The superintendent Max Grady asked Principal Robert Leo to come by the central office to meet with him.

"Mr. Grady," said Principal Leo, "we are about to have a pep rally in ten minutes. Couldn't meet you afterward?"

Mr. Grady replied, "I think it would be best if you have your assistant principals take care of the pep rally, and you come meet with me."

During the entire drive to the superintendent's office, Robert Leo racked his brain trying to think of what he had done wrong. His teacher evaluations had been turned in on time, he was on budget with the campus, and as far as he knew nothing else unusual had happened on the campus.

He knocked on the superintendent's door as soon as he got to the central office.

"Come in," said Mr. Grady. He stood up to shake the principal's hand. Several other men also stood up and shook the principal's hand. After the introductions had been made, the superintendent announced that these men were school resource officers. They were being assigned to Highview High School where Robert Leo was the principal.

"We have a suspicion that your campus is the center of something very big," said Mr. Grady.

"Andrew going to need your help."

Robert Leo furrowed his eyebrows. "Okay, what's up?"

What is the officer spoke up. "Sir, we think several of your students are involved in a sexting ring. They are Taking pictures of nude and sending them via text and uploading them into social media accounts."

Robert Leo shook his head. "Unbelievable," he said. "I have had trainings with the faculty and staff about this issue, and how to recognize it, and I've also asked the teachers to please teach mini-lessons every six weeks on why sexting is illegal and unethical. How can my campus have a sexting ring? Are you sure you have the right campus?"

The officers affirmed that they did. They had, in fact, been monitoring the situation for several months, and so far there were maybe half a dozen students involved in the operation.

The principal spoke up again, "So what's stopping you from taking the pictures from social media, and arresting the students who have done this?"

"It's not as easy as that," said the officer. "The problem is where students post these photos. They put them on social media sites that erase the photos after a certain period of time. It's been almost impossible to catch the students because there's no evidence."

The superintendent explained that the school resource officers would be around the high school campus, either inside the building or in the parking lot from time to time. In fact, the more time they spent on the campus, the more likely they would be close to catching the culprit.

"How are your teaching skills?" said Mr. Leo. "Why don't you get on the substitute list, and sub a few classes at the school? That way you'll get to meet the students, and you may even find out who's involved in the sexting ring."

The superintendent said that that was one possibility, but he wanted some of the resource officers to interview the teachers to see what they knew about the sexting that was going on on the campus.

The principal agreed to provide a spare officer for interviewing the teachers, and the meeting was over.

The next day the resource officers showed up on the campus. They had a faculty and staff roster and wanted to interview as many people as possible during their conference periods. Mr. Leo made the arrangements.

By mid-morning, the teachers were abuzz with the interviews that were going on. As each teacher had been interviewed, she or he was asked to maintain silence about the investigation.

No sooner had Ms. Coker completed her interview than she went straight to her friend's classroom. "They're finally here," she said.

Wendy Wallace looked up from her grading and said, "Who is here what are you talking about?"

"It's what I've been saying all along," said Ms. Coker. "I've thought several of the students were up to something, but I just couldn't put my finger on it. Now I know that I was right. I should have said something earlier."

Ms. Wallace assured her friend that she shouldn't blame herself. It would be best to see what the resource officers uncovered and go from there.

Within just a few days, the officers completed their investigation, and their small list of possible suspects had grown to a dozen. All of the students were sophomores and juniors, still under the age of eighteen. They had been sexting explicit photos and selling them to other students. As soon as the student making the purchase paid for the transaction, the photos were uploaded into an account in social media where they would remain for twenty-four hours. After that they disappeared. If the student wanted to see them after twenty-four hours, he or she would have to pay a second time for the photos.

The dirty dozen, the twelve boys in the sexting ring, even had a price structure for their deliverables. Photos were far less expensive than video. The most expensive video took place in the science lab between two juniors. The video was of several minutes in length, and it had been livestreamed onto the Internet by none other than Ms. Wallace.

Issue

There was a suspicion of a sexting ring at Highview High school. According to the school resource officers, an investigation has been under way for several months. All they had to do was come on campus and conduct interviews of the faculty and staff to complete their investigation.

The principal, Robert Leo, was surprised that there could be any such thing at his campus. He had specifically trained the teachers about the dangers of sexting and what to look for, and the teachers regularly taught mini-lessons in the classroom explaining why sexting is illegal.

And now this scandal was looming over the campus.

The resource officers discovered that the ring was bigger than originally thought. It was very sophisticated as well. One dozen male students were selling photos and videos, and they were posting them online after the sale.

Dilemma

Because the principal had talked about sex thing with his faculty, he had documentation with their signatures about attending the training. The teachers knew sexting was illegal, and they understood that it was their job to help prevent it.

Now one dozen sophomores and juniors were going to be arrested for running a sophisticated sexting ring. There was no doubt that other students would be implicated, either because they made purchases or because they knew about the situation and did nothing.

In addition, one of the Highview High School teachers, Wendy Wallace, will be implicated because she took several minutes of video to juniors having sex

in the science lab, and this video was included in the deliverables offered by
the sexting ring.

When Mr. Leo looked at the training sign in sheet, he noticed that Wendy
Wallace had been absent on the day of training.

Questions for Discussion

1. How should Mr. Leo let the parents know about the sexting ring?
2. How can Mr. Leo lessen the impact of love this news through social media?
3. What consequences will the boys get? What about the students who were
   complicit in the matter?
4. Can Wendy Wallace be charged with anything since she was not at the
   training and may not have known that sexting is illegal?
5. Should Mr. Leo have been investigating this issue all along?

CASE STUDY: *DRESS CODE*
SUBURBAN HIGH SCHOOL GRADES 9–12
OPERATIONS AND MANAGEMENT, 9H, L
PROFESSIONAL CAPACITY OF SCHOOL PERSONNEL, 6D

Background

Diana Stewart, principal at Garfield High School, believed in having a school
dress code. She herself had gone to a high school that had a strict dress code.
Mrs. Stewart always promised herself that when she became a principal, she
would make sure that her high school also had a dress code. She felt as though
it was one way make sure that everyone was equal regardless of their background, culture, or socioeconomic status.

Every year Mrs. Stewart reviewed the dress code with her faculty in the
spring semester. They made a list of disturbing new fashion trends they did
not want to see in the halls of their school. Often the biggest struggles happened around the skirt lengths and crop tops for the girls, and baggy pants
for the boys. At Garfield High School, these clothing items were not allowed.

During the course of the school year, the teachers wrote referrals for every
infraction of the dress code. Students were routinely sent to the assistant principal's office with the referrals. A lot of the students were considered repeat
offenders because they had the same infractions over and over. For example,
girls were frequently chastised for the length of their skirts, and they were
asked to either call home for a change of clothing, or they were sent home for
the rest of the day.

The dress code also clearly stated that no gang-style clothing was permitted.
Specifically, the dress code prohibited any closing combinations never clearly
indicative of gang affiliation. There was a population of boys who violated this

dress code policy as well. They often showed up in chinos and white T-shirts, the sleeves rolled up to reveal the boy's biceps.

Regardless of the infraction, the boys were never asked to call home for a change of clothing, nor were they ever sent home for the dress code infraction. They were told to pull up their pants, or "don't wear that again tomorrow."

Many of the girls at school noticed this inequality, and they complained about it.

At first, the girls took to social media and complained online that being asked to change clothes and getting sent home was unfair. Eventually their complaints gained traction among the students, and a movement began to treat all students fairly when it came to the dress code.

"Everyone or no one" became a common mantra at Garfield High School, and Principal Stewart had become alarmed at how vocal the girls were. When the principal met with the faculty and staff, she reminded them that students needed to be treated equitably regarding the dress code.

"If you send the girls home for infractions, you must also send the boys home," she said. "If the girls need a change of clothing, then boys who have broken the dress code policy must also have a change of clothing."

After a heated discussion, the faculty asked why the school couldn't just have uniforms.

The principal told them that uniforms were indeed a possibility, but they would have to get parents' involvement in the process. The process for moving from a dress code to school uniforms would take the entire year, but it could be done.

The faculty members formed ad hoc committees that focused on collecting research and data about school uniforms, and what types of uniforms would be most appropriate for the students at Garfield High School. And outreach committee would begin working with parents.

Over the course of the school year, Principal Stewart and her faculty held many meetings with parents, and also with the student council. The support for moving from a strict dress code to implementing a school uniform policy was surprisingly large.

Parents were relieved that they would not have to spend an exorbitant amount of money to keep their children dressed in the trendiest and most stylish clothes possible. Some of the students complained they would not be able to express their personality if they had school uniforms, but many more students indicated that they were relieved to have this huge pressure removed from daily high school life.

They admitted to spending a considerable amount of time figuring out what to wear each day for school, and some of the students who felt like they had nothing to wear or could not keep up with their peers tried to stay home or skip class.

The principal announced they would move to school uniforms the following year. At the end of the school year, parents were given a short list of appropriate clothing and suggested retailers where this clothing could be purchased.

When the new school year began, the principal and the faculty agreed that the students looked pretty sharp in their school uniforms. They were excited to be able to concentrate on instruction instead of having to constantly remind students that they were in violation of the dress code.

Just a few weeks after school had begun, however, the teachers began writing up the girls for violations of the uniform policy.

The girls had begun rolling up the waistbands of their skirts to make them shorter. Once again, the girls were being sent to the office because of showing way too much leg. The assistant principals told the girls they needed to have someone bring them other clothing or they would be sent home.

Again, when the boys pulled their uniform trousers down too low, they were told to pull them back up. They were not requested to have a change of clothing brought to them, nor were they sent home.

Another phenomenon also began to occur. The students who had previously affiliated with gangs through their clothing choices willingly wore the new school uniform, and many of the teachers were relieved about that. One teacher, in particular, though, noticed that certain gang members all wore their school uniform the same way. For example, they folded up the cuff of the left trouser leg, or they lifted their shirt collar on the right side to show their affiliation to each other and with the gang.

Issue

Garfield High School once had a stringent dress code, put into effect by school Principal Diana Stewart. When it became obvious that the dress code was more of a nuisance then an aid in class, the principal agreed to consider school uniforms. The problem with the dress code had been that students were pushing the rules to see what they could get away with.

The girls were often asked to change or were sent home, but the boys were told to make adjustments to their clothing and were allowed to stay at school.

The girls noticed this inequality and used social media to gain support and pointing it out. As a result, the faculty began to take a notice, and they felt that school uniforms were the way to go. They spent the rest of the year preparing students, their parents, and the community for the arrival of school uniforms.

Dilemma

Now that Garfield High School has school uniforms, the problems associated with the student dress code have not gone away. The principal and the faculty were certain that school uniforms would solve the problem, and yet they did not.

The girls still found ways to modify their uniforms and make them unique. Sometimes the girls shortened the length of their skirts, and there were girls who tied their school shirts into crop top shirts in order to show a little midriff.

The teachers wrote referrals for the girls, sent them to the office, and the girls either had to get change of clothing or go home. The boys who wore their pants too low were told to pull them up.

Gang members showed their affiliation to each other by the way they wore the school uniform.

Garfield High School had switched from a dress code to a uniform policy, but it seemed like nothing had changed.

Questions for Discussion

1. What was the problem with Garfield High School's dress code?
2. Explain what benefits come from having a standard dress code. What are the challenges that a dress code brings?
3. What are the benefits of having school uniforms? What are the drawbacks?
4. Why did switching to school uniforms not make a difference? Why did it not change how students were dressed?
5. In what direction should Principal Stewart lead her campus next? Should the students have uniforms or a dress code?

CASE STUDY: *OH, RATS!*
RURAL MIDDLE SCHOOL, GRADES 6–8
OPERATIONS AND MANAGEMENT, 9C
COMMUNITY OF CARE AND SUPPORT FOR STUDENTS, 5C

Background

Booker Middle School was built in the 1920s. It was an old brick building, and originally it was at the middle of nowhere, but now a small rural town had grown up around it. Booker was a fine two-story middle school, and it also had a basement which none of the other schools in the area had.

The school was originally built to serve as the district high school. When the student population grew, it also outgrew Booker, and a new flagship school was built. Booker became the middle school.

Anyone here ever worked at Booker fell in love with the campus. It was old and had plenty of the old stories to go with it. Every year people passing through the town would stop by and say, "Oh, I just had to visit." Either they had heard about the school, or they graduated with one of the earlier classes from the school.

There had been talk about tearing down the building because it was so old. There was also talk of establishing Booker Middle School as a historical site. Regardless of the decision, Booker needed a lot of TLC.

There were places where the brick crumbled away. Each principal who had been on the campus had every intention of getting repairs made, but sometimes, the budget wasn't there to do it, and other times the central office stepped in and asked the administration to wait. In the meantime, the basement developed an impressive case of mold because water drained into the basement whenever there were torrential rains. There was no place for the water to run off or to be drained out of the basement, so it was allowed to stand under the first floor until it eventually evaporated.

The first floor was as sway-backed as an old horse because the floor was so damp that it had stretched and warped. There were places someone could walk across the floor and feel as though they were sinking into the basement below.

The custodians hated changing ceiling tiles in the drop ceiling. As soon as they removed the rectangular panels, heaps and heaps of old dust and other things fell from the crawlspace above the classrooms.

One of the greatest problems that the latest principal, Ben Mulvey, faced was the lack of adequate electrical outlets. Although the campus has been upgraded over the years, the classrooms still did not have a lot of electrical outlets to operate today's modern technology. There were two plugs in every classroom, making it nearly impossible to keep computers charged and the smart boards operable.

Fortunately, a new wing had classrooms with electrical outlets. The teacher still complained, however, that they did not have enough power in the classroom.

These are not the only issues that Principal Mulvey's teachers faced.

Many of the teachers were convinced that the campus was being overrun by rats.

"Oh, that's silly," said the principal. "If we had rats, I'm sure you would see them everywhere. We may have plenty of dust and not enough electrical outlets, but we do not have rats."

To be on the safe side, the principal met with his custodial staff and asked them to place rat traps in all the classrooms. They no longer used spring traps but instead used sticky traps that were much safer and more humane.

"Please keep them hidden and out of the site of the teachers and the students," asked the principal.

After a week of having the traps set, the custodians brought in some of the traps. Sure enough, there were rats stuck in them.

The principal wrinkled his nose. "Where were the traps located?" he asked. The custodians said that most of them were from the area of the building directly over the damp basement, and three were from the kitchen.

"Tell no one," said the principal. "I will see to it that this gets taken care of."

Principal Mulvey realized that with the upcoming holiday, the district could get an extermination crew into the building to eradicate all of the rats and other vermin. It was likely that no one would ever find out.

Unfortunately, that was not the case. The rat had become emboldened even though there're people present. Sometimes the smell of food was too power-ful, and they would poke their pointy noses up from the crevices where they were hiding to sniff what delicacies awaited them.

Mrs. Long had just come back from lunch just in time to meet her sixth-period class. She was carrying the leftovers in a cardboard box and absent-mindedly set the box down all on her chair next to her desk. She got the class started on their assignment and went back to her desk to put her lunch away.

When she saw the rat, she shrieked, jumped straight up into the air, and ran out the door. Some of the kids were quick with their cell phones and captured not only their screaming teacher, but the very surprised rat in video.

By the time Mrs. Long reached Principal Mulvey's office, she was hyper-ventilating. Mr. Mulvey thought she was having a stroke and he called the nurse. When the nurse heard what had happened, she told the principal that she thought he should close the school and have it exterminated now. Any delays would jeopardize the health of the students, the faculty, and the staff even further. The principal thought about the nurse's statement. Time was also of the essence because Mr. Mulvey knew that once evidence of the rats made it to social media, his campus would be all over the news for all the wrong reasons.

Issue

Booker Middle School is a beautiful and unique old campus, but the problem is that it is old. Many of the areas in the school are in critical need of repair, and some of the repairs cannot be done without expensive and extensive work. Most of it involves a substantial disruption to instruction.

In addition to physical challenges of the building, there is also a suspicion that the building infested with rats. Mr. Mulvey, the principal, has had the bushes and other thick landscaping removed from the areas directly next to the building in hopes that the rats would not have a place to hide. However, the vermin are nesting inside the school.

Mr. Mulvey is hoping that very few people find out before he has a chance to have an extermination crew come to the building.

Dilemma

Mrs. Long, one of the teachers at Booker Middle School, is the first faculty member to see one of the rats. Many of the other faculty members had their suspicions, but now that there was video evidence circulating on the Internet of a rat enjoying the remains of Mrs. Long's lunch, the word went viral.

Not only were the teachers and the staff upset about the working conditions at Booker but the parents were upset as well. They knew that the rats could carry disease, and they did not want their children near these animals.

Mr. Mulvey, the principal, had wanted to exterminate the building during the upcoming holiday so that no one would have to miss school, and no one would be the wiser.

Now it looked as though he would have to do something sooner than later.

Questions for Discussion

1. What does Mr. Mulvey need to do on the campus for the safety of his teachers, staff, and students?
2. How do you recommend that Mr. Mulvey convince the central office that something needs to be done about the building immediately?
3. What should be done about Mrs. Long? Should Mr. Mulvey offer another classroom? Should he have replaced her lunch? Explain your rationale.
4. If the school has to close for a day in order to exterminate the building, how do you recommend that Mr. Mulvey handle social media?
5. Would it be better to wait until a longer holiday for the extermination? If so how should Mr. Mulvey handle social media?

CASE STUDY: *I SAW IT ON SOCIAL MEDIA*
RURAL MIDDLE SCHOOL GRADES 6–8
OPERATIONS AND MANAGEMENT, 9C

Background

Principal Beth Middleton looked at the list of teachers who requested a substitute for the day. Four of her teachers needed to be out, and it looked like Patty Parsons, the teacher in charge of the self-contained unit, was going to be out sick again.

There was a flu virus going around, but Mrs. Middleton thought that it had run its course. Mrs. Parsons had taken quite a few of her sick days. If memory served correctly, Mrs. Middleton recalled hearing Mrs. Parsons talking in the teachers' workroom about a cough that wouldn't go away. Whatever it was, she certainly hoped her teacher would feel better soon. No one likes getting sick.

When Mrs. Parsons returned to school, she had the same deep cough that she had before. It sounded pretty bad.

"Are you getting that checked?" asked Mrs. Middleton.

"Oh, yes, and I should have the results back very soon," coughed the teacher.

Two days later, Mrs. Parsons was in the principal's office with a piece of paper in her hands. "I think you need this," she said.

It was a doctor's note that wanted her on bed rest for the next six weeks.

"Wow," said Mrs. Middleton. "Look Patty, you have to take care of your health. You'll have to do what the doctor advises. We'll make it work out here, so don't worry about school. You might be able to use FMLA, since you worked here all past year. Have you talked to human resources (HR) yet?"

Patty assured her principal that she had. She had a full set of lesson plans prepared for each of the weeks, and her special education assistants knew how to run the classroom when a substitute would be joining them. She made her goodbyes and coughed her way out the door.

Mrs. Middleton called the HR department to confirm Mrs. Parson's leave of absence. The director said, "Yes, Mrs. Parsons had come by. Did she happen to tell the principal about her illness?"

"No," said Mrs. Middleton, "but I know that she has a horrible cough."

"She has an attorney," said the director. "She's suing the district for mold contamination."

"What?" cried out the principal. "Mrs. Parsons never said anything to me."

"She didn't have to. Remember when she wanted the air conditioning ducts cleaned? And you wouldn't do it? She says that's what gave her the cough. The doctor thinks she's allergic to mold."

The principal thought back. Yes, she did try to get the air conditioning ducts cleaned when Mrs. Parsons had asked. The district denied the request.

"Am I being sued too?" asked Mrs. Middleton.

"Probably. Welcome to administration." With that, the director hung up the phone.

Over the course of the next several days, the principal noticed mold sprouting up everywhere, it seemed. Not literally, of course, but she noticed that mold investigations in public building were news topics, and social media offered proven ways to combat mold in any environment. Mrs. Middleton wondered about the mold in her building, and what that meant for her faculty, staff, and the students.

The parents wondered, too.

They had seen the news reports, and apparently some of the same postings in social media. During the rest of the week, several of the parents asked about mold in the school building. Of course, they wanted to know that their children were safe.

"They are safe," the principal assured them.

The teachers brought up the topic of mold at lunch one day.

"You know that Mrs. Parsons may be dying," said one of them. "All because of the mold."

A parent happened to be walking past the work room at that moment. Dying? She thought. And no one is doing anything? The parent turned to her phone to publish the information. STOP THE MOLD INFESTATION AT

CARVER MIDDLE SCHOOL, she typed. Then she inserted a picture of some nasty-looking mold she found on the Internet.

Within forty-eight hours, the mold picture had been shared for more than 1200 times. Parents called the school all day, inquiring about the mold. What was the school doing about it? Could they switch schools? If their child became sick, who would pay for the medical bills?

Mrs. Middleton decided to pay to test for mold at her campus. She felt like she had to know, one way or the other. What if the rest of the teachers became ill? What if it affected students?

The mold detection company came to Carver Middle School in an unmarked van. They tested several areas in the school, including the air conditioning vents in the room where Mrs. Parsons worked.

They tested outside the building as well.

When they were finished, they returned to the principal's office.

"Well, we have your results," said the crew leader. "We found slight trace elements of mold in the air conditioning ducts, but nothing at dangerous levels. The levels are about what you'd find in any home. Pretty average. But do you want to know where the highest concentration of mold is?"

Mrs. Middleton waited.

"Outdoors. Where it's supposed to be."

"I can't control that," said Mrs. Middleton.

"Exactly."

Issue

Principal Middleton has a teacher out on FMLA, claiming that mold spores in the school building have given her a cough that she cannot seem to shake. She will be out for three weeks.

One of the parents overheard part of a conversation held by some of the teachers, and took the information out of context, and posted it in social media. The post was shared and commented on more than a thousand times.

Dilemma

Worried about being sued for doing nothing about the purported mold, Mrs. Middleton took matters into her own hands and hired a mold detection company to come out and test the campus for mold.

The company discovered only trace evidence of mold in the air conditioning ducts, and, in fact, found more mold outside the building than inside.

Mrs. Middleton now has to combat the panic on social media and let the central office know about her independent investigation.

Questions for Discussion

1. What should Mrs. Middleton do about the students and assistants in the classroom where Mrs. Parsons had become ill?
2. Should the principal be worried about the HR director's comments about being sued?
3. Should Mrs. Middleton have been informed of the situation?
4. What should Mrs. Middleton handle the social media blasts about the mold on her campus?
5. What, if anything, should Mrs. Middleton tell the central office about her decision to test for mold on the campus?

CASE STUDY: *WALK THIS WAY*
SUBURBAN HIGH SCHOOL GRADES 9–12
SCHOOL IMPROVEMENT, 10
OPERATIONS AND MANAGEMENT, 9E

Background

Principal Alexander Phillips was sure that something was afoot, but he couldn't quite put his finger on it.

Mr. Phillips never used social media. Someone on the campus had set up an account for him once, but he didn't like it, and he preferred using as old-fashioned tool for communication: face-to face communication.

When he walked into the teachers' lounge, the conversations became more subdued. Teachers looked at each other and then at their phones and then back at each other. The students, too, seemed to huddle in groups, whispering in softer tones when he walked by. They too relied on their phones for up-to-the-minute's messages.

Principal Phillips shrugged it off, thinking he would find out sooner or later what everyone was up to.

It turned out that he found out sooner, and he didn't like it.

In February, as a protest of new immigration policies in the United States, many people had planned "A Day without Immigrants." The idea was to show how important immigration was to the United States. America couldn't function without immigrants who were doing the jobs that most citizens didn't want to do. That meant laborers and other hourly employees with immigrant status would not go to work that day. They planned to stay home to show how important they were to the economy and to business in general.

The idea gained traction in a variety of arenas, including schools. If enough students stayed home, the school would receive less money in attendance. If they received less money, they would notice the absence of the immigrants. Capitalists always noticed money, especially if they weren't getting any of it. Nothing like hurting them in the pocketbook was the general consensus about "A Day without Immigrants."

Like the rest of their families, the students who were immigrants decided that they, too, would hold a walkout. Their walkout would be at school. They organized the event using only social media.

On "A Day without Immigrants," the teachers at Milburne High School reported for work as always. They signed in, got coffee, and got in line in front of the copier machines to prepare for the day ahead. Many were anxious to see what the day had in store for them.

When the attendance reporting was complete at 10:00 a.m., Principal Phillips was shocked at the number in front of him: 49 percent. The Milburne High School's average daily attendance rate was 94 percent. This new number had been nearly slashed in half.

Good grief, thought Principal Phillips. Are there really that many immigrant students at my campus?

"Best day EVER," thought some of the Milburne teachers.

Five teachers began posting their thoughts on their favorite social media platform:

"Wow, zero discipline problems!"
"Less crowded classrooms!"
"First time I could teach the entire lesson without disruption!"

"Thanks President Trump! I love teaching again!"
"OMG! Can we please do this again tomorrow?"
The teachers later retracted their statements, but it was too late.

The threads were public, and some of their students read them. So did their parents and some advocacy groups.

The district policy for social media was to allow teachers and students to share information across social media platforms, but anything said had to be positive. There could be no targeting, and no negative comments.

Students took screenshots of the teachers' comments, and when they returned to school the next day, they cored the colors of the Mexican flag, spoke only in Spanish to their teachers, and showed the teachers the printed comments from social media.

"How can we ever trust you or respect you again?" the students asked.

"What about us?" asked the teachers. "It seems like as long as our opinions are aligned with liberal dissenters, we can say what we want. We can't state an opinion if it is not aligned to the liberal agenda. Conservative teachers, and there are some of us, have rights, too."

The school district was planning an investigation of each teacher who had negative things to say about "A Day without Immigrants," and the district also planned to take corrective action.

They began by requiring every teacher to retract their statements and make a public apology for their inappropriate statements in social media.

Mr. Phillips resigned himself to writing up his teachers for their public comments, but he understood where they were coming from. Who wouldn't like smaller class sizes, regardless of the reason? Of course, smaller class sizes meant fewer discipline problems and less wear and tear of the building. That made total sense.

What didn't make sense to Mr. Phillips was that teachers were not allowed to state dissenting opinions.

Issue

"A Day without Immigrants" affected the schools as much as it affected the workplace. At least half the population at one high school skipped class that day in favor of a walkout. The idea was to prove that every business, including schools, needed immigrants.

The teachers felt otherwise, and they were delighted to work in conditions where they said that the classrooms were not overcrowded, the building stayed cleaner, and there were fewer discipline problems.

Then they posted their thoughts in social media.

The students and their parents saw these posts and were shocked at how some of their favorite teachers felt.

Dilemma

Mr. Phillips has to write up the five teachers who dissented with "A Day without Immigrants" by noting in social media how nice it was not to have the students in school. While Principal Phillips knows that the teachers violated the acceptable use policy that they agreed upon becoming employed by the district, he also knew that the teachers were not allowed to freely speak their minds in social media, although more liberal teachers could do so.

Although the teachers had alienated their students and the community, Mr. Phillips debated whether he should follow through with reprimanding his teachers.

Questions for Discussion

1. Do teachers have the right to dissent politically in public forums? Why or why not?
2. What should the high school do regarding the absent students? Should they face consequences? If so, what?

3. Can the district demand retraction in social media?
4. How can Mr. Phillips unite the school and the community?
5. What advice would you give Mr. Phillips about his final thoughts?

CASE STUDY: *CHARGE IT*
URBAN HIGH SCHOOL
OPERATIONS AND MANAGEMENT, 9D
ETHICS AND PROFESSIONAL NORMS, 2A

Background

Roy Sanchez was the newly appointed principal at One Fine Charter School, an urban high school in the city.

Mr. Sanchez was ecstatic about becoming a principal at a charter campus. He knew far too well that in traditional schools, processes were slow and cumbersome, and bureaucratic red tape could prevent a principal and the teachers from doing the things that he needed to do as quickly as he needed to do them.

Public charter schools were meant to change all that. They operated in a fast and fluid environment, often outside many of the district policies and procedures that tended to bog down instruction.

One Fine Charter School was located in his own district, where Roy Sanchez had been both a teacher and an assistant principal. He was the perfect fit because of his love for doing the right things for students and because he had worked for a long time in the district. He knew how the district did business. The district created the charter campus in order to provide an educational environment far different from what their traditional high schools provided students, and this way, the district didn't lose any enrollment.

When the district administration met with Principal Sanchez, they told him that he pretty much had carte blanche to do whatever it was necessary to help children learn. The goal was to get high school students back on track with their credits so that they could graduate and either enter the workforce or continue their education.

Principal Sanchez wanted One Fine Charter to be the kind of high school kids were eager to attend and be proud of graduating from. He would have to do a lot to make that happen, though. The district placed the charter school in their oldest, smallest, ugliest available building. It was surrounded by sprawling, sad-looking portables connected to the main building with a leaking roof, cracked and uneven sidewalks. The main building of the school was tiny; getting to the classrooms involved a considerable amount of walking.

The furniture for One Fine Charter consisted of a ragtag collection of hand-me-downs from other campuses. It seemed like no two chairs were alike, and much of it had graffiti older than some of the students who would be using it. The walls inside the building were drab and faded, and those inside the portables were scarred. The principal's office consisted of a folding chair and a student desk.

None of this was okay.

Principal Sanchez had heard about how nimble and agile charter schools could be when designing instruction and acquiring the things students and teachers needed, and he was about to put it to test. The district had issued him a purchase card so that he could purchase what his campus needed when they needed it.

He had no time to delay.

With eager anticipation, the principal locked the building and drove to the nearest wholesale club, where he opened up an account for the school.

After four hours of shopping, Principal Sanchez was exhausted and finished. He took as many of the purchases as he could with him, and he arranged to have some of the others delivered to the campus. Then he set about getting the campus ready for the beginning of school. He worked numerous long hours scrubbing, cleaning, and painting the school. He wanted the teachers and students alike to be pleased with their new environment. They were. Principal Sanchez hosted a lovely back-to-school celebration for his teachers, students, and their parents. He and the faculty grilled burgers and hotdogs, and everyone got to know each other a little better.

One Fine Charter was going to really be different, thought the students and their parents.

When it came time to turn in receipts and documentation, Principal Sanchez realized that finance coding of all purchases allowed for a consistent way to identify what was purchased and with what funds. Principal Sanchez turned in this itemized report in September for his purchases.

Upon receiving the documentation, the finance director called the superintendent, who in turn called Principal Sanchez to the central office building. The superintendent wanted to meet with the principal about the expenditures that had come in on the first charge receipt—for nearly $35,000.

Issue

The urban school district created a charter campus within its boundaries for the purpose of keeping their student enrollment up. The district assigned a campus principal to an unused building and told him to get everything ready for school. They also gave him a purchase card.

The principal used the charge card to charge $35,000 worth of materials and other goods for the campus needs, illustrated by table 9.1.

Dilemma

The finance director and the superintendent have seen the charges, and now they wanted to talk to Principal Sanchez, in person. The charges were outrageous, and several were inappropriate. They wanted answers.

"A golf cart?? A wine cooler?" asked the superintendent. He threw the report down on his desk and glowered at the principal. "What were you thinking? No, let me guess—you weren't thinking!"

Mr. Sanchez cleared his throat. "I was thinking I would reimburse the district for the wine cooler. It's not like that was for my office or anything. It was on sale, so I went ahead and picked it up rather than drive home to get my personal club card. I must have forgotten to attach the check for the reimbursement."

Table 9.1   Sample expense report on Principal Sanchez' purchases.

Item(s)	Amount	Object Classification
14 boxes of paper (6 reams in a box)	255.00	Supplies & materials
1 laser jet printer	649.00	Supplies & materials
Toner, black	162.00	Supplies & materials
Toner, color	264.00	Supplies & materials
10 variety packs of chips (snacks)	128.00	Incentives
5 bags chocolates	107.00	Incentives
1 pair rain boots	84.00	Incentives
Shoe polishing machine	72.00	Admin office
Outdoor pavilion	499.00	Incentives
Golf cart with weather shield	2899.00	Admin office
Student chairs (100)	16,978.00	Classroom
20 gallons paint, assorted colors + brushes/rollers	1,200.00	Classroom
Gasoline	438.00	Travel
Desk and hutch	906.00	Admin office
Leather office chair	275.00	Admin office
Folding tables	1310.00	Classroom
Wine cooler	279.00	Supplies & materials
Toilet paper	24.00	Supplies & materials
Large stainless grill	5,644.00	Incentives
Hamburgers, hotdogs, buns	301.00	Incentives
Highlighters, pens, pencils, dry erase markers	413.00	Supplies & materials
NSAID pain reliever, 500 ct.	12.00	Supplies & materials
Popcorn machine	1795.00	Incentives
Scrolling message sign	197.00	Admin office
Total	34,891.00	

Questions for Discussion

1. What should the principal have done before purchasing all of these items with the purchase card?
2. Is it okay to charge items for personal use and then reimburse the district later?
3. Which items would be considered inappropriate for school business?
4. Which items should the principal go through the school district for? Why?
5. Can the superintendent require the principal to take these items back? Why or why not?

Chapter 10

Continuous School Improvement

CASE STUDY: *IN HER OWN HANDS*
SUBURBAN MIDDLE SCHOOL, GRADES 9–12
SCHOOL IMPROVEMENT, 10H

Background

Annie Sloan was a seventh grade student at Creek Middle School. This magnet school, located in the suburbs, appealed to a particular group of students and their parents. Creek Middle School focused exclusively on academics. There were no athletic programs or other distractions that could deter her students from keeping their eyes on core subjects and a few related electives, such as career and technology courses and advanced social sciences.

The academic work was grueling, and students worked hard not only at school but also when completing hours of homework each night and on the weekends. It was a privilege to be selected to attend the school, and students didn't want to lose their seat at Creek Middle School. In fact, very little could make a student withdraw from the prestigious magnet school.

The school boasted a tight-knit community based on support and respect for each other. One of the best clubs to belong to on the campus was the Nerd Club. This club's membership helped each other understand some more difficult concepts they learned about in class, and they also served as tutors for the other students on campus.

Annie Sloan was in her second year of membership in the Nerd Club. This year she was the club secretary, and she was hoping that next year she could be the vice president and president of the club. She loved working with other students and was always eager to help out where she could. She knew a lot of the students and the other grade levels because of her tutoring work, and most of them liked her gregarious personality.

Rusty Banks, one of the eighth graders, also liked Annie Sloan. He asked her to go around a couple of times when she was tutoring him in math, but Annie politely turned him down.

Rusty's friends laughed at him, and teased him.

"What's the matter Rusty, did someone finally tell you NO?" they chortled.

More determined than ever, Rusty decided that he would get Annie's attention, and that she would want to go out with him.

One morning when Annie was passing him in the hallway, Rusty reached out to try to pat her bottom. The hallway was crowded and Annie couldn't be sure if the touching was accidental or on purpose. On another occasion, when the hall with less crowded, Rusty tried to pat her on the bottom again.

This time Annie knew it was intentional. She told her teacher about what had happened, but the teacher dismissed the incident, saying that sometimes these things happen.

A couple of weeks later, Rusty tried catching Annie again. She was putting books into her locker when Rusty came up and put his hand on the locker door. The back of his hand gently brushed against Annie's rib cage. Then he moved his hands as though he was going to touch her breasts.

Annie quickly moved away, slammed her locker shut and told Rusty to stop it. Then she went to the counselor's office. Annie told the counselor what had just happened, but the but the counselor said there was nothing that could be done because there were no witnesses.

Mad and frustrated, Annie back to her class. When Rusty tried something like this again, she wanted to be ready. Annie thought for a long time about what her next course of action should be, especially since none of the adults seemed interested in helping her out.

The following week, Annie was getting a drink of water from the water fountain, and Rusty came up behind her, and pushed against her with his hips. Annie stood up.

She knew instantly that this was the time to take action. She reached up behind him, grabbed Rusty's head from behind, as though pulling him closer, and then quickly stepped out of the way as she slammed his head into the water fountain. The spigot caught him just above the eye and the lacerated Rusty's eyebrow.

Rusty howled in pain, and blood gushed from his forehead. Annie's eyes widened at the amount of blood that relentlessly spilled out, but she held her resolve and stared Rusty down. "Serves you right," she said.

One of the assistant principals saw what Annie had done, and he took her to his office after sending Rusty to the nurses for first aid.

This assistant principal allowed Annie to write a statement of what had happened and he had her date and sign the document. Then he told her that she would be suspended the following day for assaulting another student.

At the news of being suspended from school, Annie broke down in tears, trying to explain that she had been assaulted all along, and no one would help her with the problem. The assistant principal said it didn't matter; he saw what she had done. She injured another student on campus, and there was no tolerance for her behavior. The schools rules said that she had to be suspended.

"What about Rusty? What consequence does he get for trying to grope me in public?" Annie asked.

"Rusty said he didn't do anything," said the assistant principal.

Annie stayed home the next day because of this suspension she had received as a consequence for taking matters into her own hands. Her mother was a school principal in another school district, and she made it a point to be at the principal's office at Creek Middle School first thing in the morning.

"I'd like to see Mr. Robert Meeks, the principal," said Mrs. Sloan.

The office worker asked if Mrs. Sloan had an appointment with the principal. Mrs. Sloan said that she did not, but that the principal would definitely want to meet with her.

"May I ask what this is in regard to?" said the office worker.

"Yes," said Mrs. Sloan, "you may tell your principal that I am here to meet with him about a Title IX violation, and I expected he will want to meet with me before I meet with media."

Issue

A seventh grade girl has repeatedly been assaulted by an eighth grade boy in the public areas of Creek Middle School. Each time the assaults have become physically more aggressive, more threatening and more blatant.

After each incident, the seventh grader tried telling an adult in the building about what had happened, but no one took her seriously. The assistant principal who saw the seventh grader injure the eighth grader at the water fountain allowed the student to write down her version of what happened, but he did not question her or investigate the story. Instead, he suspended her from school.

He sided with the male student who assaulted her.

Dilemma

The seventh grade student's mother is a school principal in a nearby school district, and she wants to meet with the principal about "a Title IX violation" that occurred on his campus.

The principal, Mr. Meeks, has been taken by surprise about the parent's request. He tries to delay the meeting for a few minutes to find out exactly what happened yesterday, but no one is in the assistant principal's office at the moment.

He will have to meet with the irate mother and find out from her what happened and then follow up with his campus personnel later.

The Creek Middle School principal and Mrs. Sloan have never met before, but Mrs. Sloan is eager to meet the principal and find out why her daughter was denied due process and suspended anyway, when all along Annie Sloan was a victim of sexual harassment.

Questions for Discussion

1. What do you think of the way the assistant principal reacted? How should the assistant principal have handled the assault?
2. Why would Mrs. Sloan think her daughter had been denied due process? Is she right?
3. Mrs. Sloan complained that her daughter was a party to a Title IX violation. Is she right? Why do you think she used this phrase for her meeting with the principal?
4. Was the suspension for injuring another student fair and just, even if the perpetrator had been victimized? Why or why not?
5. Principal Robert Meeks will need to investigate the situation. Who are some of the people he should speak with?

CASE STUDY: *FLIPPED OUT*
SUBURBAN HIGH SCHOOL GRADES 9–12
SCHOOL IMPROVEMENT, 10A, B
CURRICULUM, INSTRUCTION, AND ASSESSMENT, 4C

Background

The teachers at Browning High School always liked to try innovative strategies in their classrooms. It was important to them that they were on the cutting edge of new education initiatives. During the course of one school year, many of the teachers attended training about the flipped classroom.

The premise of the flipped classroom was that students did the initial preparation for class at home. They would listen to lectures, engage in advance reading, and complete any other activities they would need to have complete before participating in the guided practice assignment or independent practice assignment back at school the next day.

The teachers loved this idea.

They could prepare all of the instruction materials and their notes, and then send these home with the students so that the time in class would be devoted to collaborative learning at its best. In preparation for the year of flipped instruction, the teachers made podcasts of their lectures, or they recorded them on DVDs, and they made extensive notes for the students to take home.

The teachers also planned engaging in activities for the classroom. To the teachers, it seemed as though the flipped classroom would double the amount of instructional time they had. The entire faculty was in support of creating flipped classrooms for instruction. It wasn't too often that the faculty and staff at Browning High School agreed on anything, so the principal agreed that the teachers could implement this new approach.

Principal George Garza cautioned his teachers, however, that for the school to engage in flipped classrooms schoolwide, the teachers would have to prove that this new instructional strategy worked for all of the students. It would not be okay for one particular strategy to benefit only some of the students. It has to be effective for all of the students, not just some.

The first few weeks were promising. The energy about school was high, and students were genuinely excited to be back in class and with their friends. They especially liked the class projects because they were hands-on and required extensive collaboration, which meant that the students could socialize with each other while working on the class projects.

The first six weeks went very well. Even students who traditionally performed poorly in the classroom had much better grades than in the past. Flipped classroom instruction was working!

During the second six weeks, however, the momentum seemed to lag just a little bit. Some of the students were not getting their pre-activities done. They skipped the reading or forgot to listen to the lectures. At first, they could fake it in the classroom, and still participate in the hands-on activities. It wasn't long before the lack of preparation became obvious.

The teachers at Browning High School began to complain that students weren't getting their homework done.

Just after the second progress report window, the school held an open house. The principal agreed to let several of the teachers present at short meeting before the open house to show parents what flipped classrooms were and why they were so effective.

The parents aren't having any of it, however. As soon as the teachers began their presentation, there were already rumblings and grumblings about this new initiative.

Parents said they didn't like it because the students had to do all of the hard learning at home by themselves. It wasn't like the parents could help them learn some of these concepts, like the new math. That was supposed to be the teachers' job, and the parents didn't appreciate having to do the teachers' work for them.

Furthermore, they complained that some of the teachers were preventing the students from participating in the classroom activities during the day because they had not done their assignments the previous evening. The teachers were using the class time for students to catch up and complete their homework assignments. As a result, the teachers had to spend time explaining the concepts to the students who didn't do their homework while trying to lead the hands-on activity with the other students.

The parents of those students who were completing their homework became frustrated that their children were being held back by those who were not. Parents whose children were not doing the assignments complained that the teachers were not helping their children learn.

"What are we paying you for, if you are not going to teach?" they said. "I pay good money in taxes to pay your salary, and you don't even want to work for it."

The teachers didn't know what to say. The principal stepped in, took the microphone, and addressed the parents.

"The flipped classroom strategy," he said, "is the new initiative that expand the timing class by having students listen to lectures do preparatory work before the actual learning takes place. The teachers here at Browning High School worked very hard to be prepared with the strategy. Your children need to work just as hard in completing their assignments."

Some of the parents tried to explain that students actually had less time in the evenings now because of the flipped classroom initiative.

"Our kids have to do the preparation for all of their content classes, and it takes a lot of time. Some of the kids are in athletics or extra-curriculars, or they have a job. They do not have the time to do this much work in preparation for their classes."

Principal Garza promised that he would look at the matter and hold another parent meeting just for those parents who are concerned about flipped classroom instruction. In the meantime, he wanted to take a closer look at the data and then meet with his faculty.

Issue

The Browning High School teachers loved the idea of flipped classroom instruction. They wanted to implement this initiative right away, and they wanted it to be campus wide. In preparation for the new instructional approach, they worked throughout the summer to prepare their material.

At first, the flipped classroom approach worked perfectly. The students were doing the preparation at home, and teachers could actually teach. There were so excited. For many of them, this was the reason they got into education in the first place.

Teachers modified the material that were going home for students, so that students at all levels and abilities could access them. It took a little more work, but the teachers felt it was worth the work because of the excitement about classroom instruction.

Dilemma

The parents did not feel the same way the teachers felt. In fact, many parents were concerned that the teachers were creating an unnecessary burden on the high school students who had things to do. In addition, the teachers were sending their work home for the parents to do with the students instead of the teachers providing instruction in the classroom. To the parents at Browning High School, flipped instruction made no sense. Instead, it made them feel as though the teachers were not doing their jobs.

Questions for Discussion

1. What problem did the flipped classroom approach create? How could it have been circumvented?
2. Should the principal have permitted 100 percent of the teachers on his campus to flip their classrooms? Why or why not?
3. Why are grades alone not a measure of the students' abilities or achievement?
4. Recommend a better way to implement a new instructional strategy on the campus.
5. How could parents have been involved in the flipped classroom approach from the beginning? Why was their support necessary?
6. Describe ways that the school could have used social media to support a new campus initiative.

CASE STUDY: *SANCTUARY SCHOOL*
SUBURBAN HIGH SCHOOL GRADES 9–12
SCHOOL IMPROVEMENT, 10A
PROFESSIONAL COMMUNITY FOR TEACHERS AND STAFF, 7D

Background

Principal Ruben Sanchez was living the American dream. He grew up poor, spent a decade teaching social studies in middle school, and now was the principal of a large-sized high school in Meadow Bend. The school was a large suburban campus that provided instruction for several thousand students.

Sanchez had several assistant principals and counselors to help them with the needs of the students and the teachers. As a team, they took care of instruction, operations, transportation, and safety on campus. It was a big job, but everybody liked pitching in to help make the campus a great environment for learning.

The student population was 30 percent African American, 30 percent white, and 40 percent Hispanic. Of the Hispanic students, 11 percent were English language learners and 23 percent were classified migrant students, because either they or their family traveled in search of seasonal work. Constantly changing schools made it especially difficult on migrant students. Their English language skills were far weaker than those of their peers, and they often enrolled in a new school that was that an entirely different place in the curriculum. The constant changes made keeping up with school work difficult.

Ruben Sanchez himself knew what it was like to be a child of immigrant parents. As a young boy in grade school, Ruben traveled with his family as a migrant worker. He too had difficulties keeping up with his school work, and he was often asked to work in the fields alongside his parents because scraping out a living was more important than the luxury of an education.

When Ruben's parents were finally able to settle in one place, Ruben was able to focus on his school. He was awarded a scholarship to the local university, and he went into education because he wanted immigrant students to have an easier time of transitioning into a school environment than he had ever had. He wanted to give it back to the community.

Principal Sanchez made it a point to welcome every new immigrant family to his campus, and he always checked on the students who were immigrants to make sure they had what they needed to be successful in high school. Sometimes that meant giving the students the paper and pens that they needed for class work, and sometimes it meant looking the other way when they lost a textbook or a library book.

"They understand the value of a book, and what is inside it," said Principal Sanchez. "How amazing that a child would steal a book to take with him on his journeys. There are worse things to be stealing, you know."

Ruben Sanchez's love for immigrant students was well known in the community. Some of the parents greatly appreciated his willingness to take a stance and help students who needed the most. Others were adamant that the money spent on immigrants should be spent on other American students who already lived in the community and went to the school.

One of the parents, Louise Hesse, started a blog outlining all of the problems created by immigrant students. At first, her target was Meadow Brook High School. Eventually, she began reporting on the incidents that happened across the state and beyond if they involved immigrant students. She was particularly vocal about the illegal immigrants living in the country and receiving what was, in her eyes, a free education.

"Shameful, downright shameful," she wrote on her webpage. Many of the parents from Meadow Brook High School followed her.

The campus was a busy place, and no administrator could be visible all the time. Neither could the teachers. Even though they were supposed to be in the halls between class transition times, the teachers were also trying to get ready for their next class in the short break between two periods.

Perhaps that's why no one saw one student still lingering in the hallway when the bell rang. Nellie Mace had to go back to her locker in D Hall because she forgot the homework she was supposed to bring to her class in B Hall.

"Better to get a tardy then zero on the homework," she thought. She headed back the way she had come, intent on making it back to class as quickly as she could.

Unfortunately, she never made it back to class. No one saw the other two students who were following her down the hall. They caught up with her and flanked her on either side before pushing her into the girls' restroom.

It was another student who found Nelly in the restroom, where she was sobbing heavily. Natalie's clothes had been torn. The student took her to the counselor's offices.

Nelly reported that she has been raped. When asked if she knew who her assailants were, she assured them that she did. There were two of the students from her class; both of them were immigrants from Central America. She was also aware that both boys were in the country illegally.

It didn't take long for Louise has to catch hold of news and make a post about it on her blog page. "And this is the reason," she wrote, "that we do not need illegal immigrants in our country. Deport them all before they commit another crime."

The principal was furious about what he had read on the parent's blog, but Mr. Sanchez was even more angry when instead of the local police, officers from Immigration and Customs Enforcement (ICE) came to pick up the two boys. The principal was upset that they would come to the school to make the arrest, but he was also hot about the incident so quickly centering around immigration.

The principal told the officers from ICE that there was no proof that the boys had done anything, and that he personally thought they were there to pick on these students based on their last names and countries of origin.

The principal expressly forbade the officers to step beyond the administration office to arrest the students.

"This is a sanctuary school," said Principal Sanchez, "and you may not pass."

Issue

The campus principal has a special affinity for immigrant students because he himself once worked as an immigrant in the American fields. Principal Sanchez would like to provide all immigrants at this school a better opportunity than he had when he was in an American school. One of the parents whose child attends the school is an avid proponent of deporting illegal immigrants. She feels as though these students did not deserve an American education because they're in the country illegally.

When two illegal immigrants rape one of the students in the girls' bathroom during class, Principal Sanchez denied access to his school or the students. He refused to permit the ICE agents to come onto his campus to arrest the boys.

Dilemma

There is already dissention in the community about the presence of illegal immigrants, and all immigrants, whether here legally or illegally, are concerned for their own safety.

A female student at the high school has been raped by two male illegal immigrant students. No one saw the boys escort her to a bathroom, but she was found later and taken to the counselor's office for attention. The raped student reveals that she knew the names of attackers, and that she could identify them.

It was not that the police came to arrest the two boys. Four officers from ICE came to the campus to arrest the boys.

Mr. Ruben Sanchez, the principal, declared his campus a sanctuary school, where no one may come in to arrest or otherwise detain illegal immigrants. If needed, he would allow the boys to spend the night in his school so that they would remain protected from harm.

Questions for Discussion

1. Can Mr. Sanchez declare his campus sanctuary school? Why or why not?
2. Does he have the right to provide safe harbor to the two illegal immigrants who committed a crime? Does he have to provide them an education at all?
3. Does Louise Hess have the right to post her opinions about the illegal immigrants on her blog? Why or why not?
4. How did the principal allow his personal background to influence his decision regarding immigrant students at his campus?
5. How would you suggest that Principal Sanchez advocate for the education of illegal immigrants in the high school?

Bibliography

Note: Some of the case studies in this book are based on relevant and timely articles in the news media.

Alvarez, B. (January 2016). "Girls Fight Back against Gender Bias in School Dress Codes." *NEA Today*. Retrieved from: http://neatoday.org/2016/01/06/school-dress-codes-gender-bias/

American Civil Liberties Union. (n.d.). "Know Your Rights: LGBT High School Students—What to Do If You Face Harassment at School." American Civil Liberties Union. Retrieved from: http://www.aclu.org/know-your-rights/lgbt-high-school-students-what-do-if-you-face-harassment-school

Amiri, C. (March 28, 2017). "Oakland Baseball Players Accused of Racist Social Media Posts." Fox Television Stations. Retrieved from: http://www.fox2detroit.com/news/local-news/244547466-story

Andone, D. (March 9, 2017). "School Prom Dress Guide Draws Body-Shaming Accusations." CNN. Retrieved from: http://www.cnn.com/2017/03/08/us/high-school-prom-dress-guide/

Anti-Defamation League. (2015). "Religion in the Public Schools. Anti-Defamation League." Retrieved from: http://www.adl.org/assets/pdf/civil-rights/religiousfreedom/rips/rips-update-0715/RIPS-CH13-DressCodes.pdf

Aviles, C. (February 21, 2014). "The Flipped Classroom Is a Lie." *Teched Up Teacher*. Retrieved from: http://www.techedupteacher.com/the-flipped-classroom-is-a-lie/

Bethany. (January 12, 2017). Neo-Nazi Instagram Account Spreads around Saratoga High School. WGNA. Retrieved from: http://wgna.com/neo-nazi-instagram-account-spreads-around-saratoga-high-school/

Bowie, L. (March 23, 2015). "Students Cheated by Posting Test Questions on Social Media." *Baltimore Sun*. Retrieved from: http://www.baltimoresun.com/news/maryland/bs-md-test-cheating-20150322-story.html

Brennan, C. (December 20, 2016). "Ohio Teacher Disciplined for Algebra Lesson About Sexting 'Nudes.'" *NY Daily News*. Retrieved from: http://www.nydailynews.com/

news/national/ohio-teacher-disciplined-sexting-themed-algebra-lesson -article-1.2917919

De Los Santos, B., Anderson, T., and Krishnakumar, P. (February 3, 2017). "'We've Woken Up': What It's Like to Be LGBT under Trump." *LA Times*. Retrieved from: http://www.latimes.com/projects/la-na-lgbt-voices-trump/

Eldridge, E. (March 26, 2017). Students Complain of Rat Infestation in High School. AJC. Retrieved from: http://www.ajc.com/news/local/students-complain-rat-infesta tion-high-school/3qLaGeCWUqdUe64YOt2KcO/

Fox News. (October 14, 2003). Should a High School Principal Have Been Arrested? Fox News, *The O'Reilly Factor*. Retrieved from: http://www.foxnews.com/ story/2003/10/14/should-high-school-principal-have-been-arrested.html

Haines, A. (October 31, 2016). Mom of Teen Banned from All Schools Files Human Rights Complaint. *City News*. Retrieved from: http://www.citynews.ca/2016/10/31/ mom-teen-banned-schools-files-human-rights-complaint/

Hanna, L. (January 29, 2016). 3 Connecticut High School Students Charged Following Sexting Scandal That Involved 50 Teens. *NY Daily News*. Retrieved from: http://www.nydailynews.com/news/national/connecticut-high-school-pupils -charged-sexting-scandal-article-1.2513438

Hattie, J. (2012). *Visible Learning for Teachers: Maximizing Impact on Learning*. London: Routledge.

Higbea, M. R. (January 1, 1970). He Who Does the Talking, Does the Learning. *Making Teaching Visible*. Retrieved from http://making-teaching-visible.blogspot. com/2015/11/he-who-does-talking-does-learning.html

Hoft, J. (February 4, 2017). Middle School Student Attacked on Bus for Wearing Trump #MAGA Hat—Then School Suspends Him. *The Gateway Pundit*. Retrieved from: http://www.thegatewaypundit.com/2017/02/middle-school-student-attacked-bus-wearing-trump-maga-hat-schools-suspends-video/

Hozien, W. (2017). *Elementary School Principals in Action Resolving Case Studies in Leadership*. Lanham, MD: Rowman and Littlefield.

Human Rights Watch. (December 7, 2016). Like Walking through a Hailstorm. Human Rights Watch. Retrieved from: http://www.hrw.org/report/2016/12/07/ walking-through-hailstorm/discrimination-against-lgbt-youth-us-schools

Grynbaum, M. M. and Otterman, S. (March 4, 2015). "New York City Adds 2 Muslim Holy Days to Public School Calendar." *NY Times*. Retrieved from: http:// www.nytimes.com/2015/03/05/nyregion/new-york-to-add-two-muslim-holy-days -to-public-school-calendar.html?_r=0

Hattie, J. (2012). *Visible Learning for Teachers: Maximizing Impact on Learning*. London: Routledge.

"Title IX." (n.d.). *Know Your IX* (website). Retrieved from: http://www.knowyourix .org/college-resources/title-ix/

Martin, E. (February 16, 2017). "District Investigating Social Media Posts in Which Riverside Teachers Disparaged Students Absent for 'Day Without Immigrants.'" *KTLA*. Retrieved from: http://ktla.com/2017/02/16/jurupa-valley -school-district-investigating-teachers-who-disparaged-students-participating-in -day-without-immigrants-on-social-media/

Nadolny, T. L. (June 1, 2016). "Philadelphia Schools Add Two Muslim Holidays." *Philly*. Retrieved from: http://www.philly.com/philly/education/20160601_Phila delphia_schools_add_two_Muslim_holidays.html

"School Uniforms as an Anti-Gang Tactic". (June 30, 2014). National Crime Prevention Council. Retrieved from: http://ncpc.typepad.com/prevention_works_blog/2014/06/ school-uniforms-as-an-anti-gang-tactic.html

National Policy Board for Educational Administration (2015). *Professional Standards for Educational Leaders 2015*. Reston, VA: Author. Retrieved from http:// npbea.org/wp-content/uploads/2017/06/Professional-Standards-for-Educational-Leaders_2015.pdf

"The Top 10 Questions Parents Have About the Flipped Classroom—And How to Answer Them." (August 9, 2016). *Panopto*. Retrieved from: https://www.panopto. com/blog/the-top-10-questions-parents-have-about-the-flipped-classroom-and -how-to-answer-them/

Reicher, M. (May 22, 2016). "Special Report: LA Charter School Under Review After Principal Charges $100K." *LA Daily News*. Retrieved from http://www. dailynews.com/social-affairs/20160522/special-report-la-charter-school -under-review-after-principal-charges-100k

Rocha, V. (June 29, 2016). "Bay Area School Threatened After Teacher Clashes with Neo-Nazis at State Capitol." *LA Times*. Retrieved from: http://www.latimes.com/local/ lanow/la-me-ln-bay-area-school-threat-neo-nazi-20160629-snap-htmlstory.html

Salinas, R. (August 22, 2016). "San Antonia-Area Schools with the Most Bullying, Harassment Complaints in 2014–15." *My San Antonio*. Retrieved from: http:// www.mysanantonio.com/news/education/article/San-Antonio-schools-bullying -harassment-claims-6836673.php

Simpson, M. (2010). "Social Networking Nightmares." *NEA*. Retrieved from: http:// www.nea.org/home/38324.htm

Smith, J. (October 12, 2016). "Teenage 'Fuhrer' of Neo-Nazi Facebook Page Where High School Students Talked about 'Hanging Jews on Trees' Commits Suicide 'to Show Allegiance to the Group.'" *Daily Mail*. Retrieved from: http:// www.dailymail.co.uk/news/article-3835259/Teenage-Fuhrer-neo-Nazi-Facebook -page-high-school-students-talked-hanging-African-Jews-trees-commits-suicide -allegiance-group.html

Sokmensuer, H. (March 20, 2017). "Ex-Teacher Allegedly 'Groomed' Missing 15-Year-Old Student Who May Have Disappeared with Him." Yahoo. Retrieved from: https://www.yahoo.com/celebrity/ex-teacher-allegedly-groomed-missing -231215551.html

Stokes, P. (November 30, 2016). "Bullied Alabama Teen Returns to School, Principal Placed on Administrative Leave." *AL*. Retrieved from: http://www.al.com/news/ mobile/index.ssf/2016/11/bullied_alabama_teen_returns_t.html

"Facts about Bullying." (October 14, 2014). *Stop Bullying*. Retrieved from: https:// www.stopbullying.gov/media/facts/index.html

Tchekmedyian, A. (March 7, 2017). "'A Day without a Women' for Many Means a Day Without School." *LA Times*. Retrieved from: http://www.latimes.com/ nation/la-na-day-without-women-20170307-story.html

Wadsworth, C. (February 9, 2017). "Loudoun County Students Plan Walkout Friday." *The Burn*. Retrieved from: http://www.theburn.com/2017/02/09/opinion-loudoun-county-students-plan-protest-friday/

Westervelt, E. (September 15, 2016). "Frustration. Burnout. Attrition. It's Time to Address the National Teacher Shortage." *NPR*. Retrieved from: http://www.npr.org/sections/ed/2016/09/15/493808213/frustration-burnout-attrition-its-time-to-address-the-national-teacher-shortage

Zimmerman, M. (March 20, 2017). "New Details Emerge in Alleged School Rape of Teen by Illegal Immigrants." *Fox News*. Retrieved from: http://www.foxnews.com/us/2017/03/20/maryland-girl-allegedly-raped-in-high-school-bathroom-by-two-teens-at-least-one-here-illegally.html

About the Author

Dr. Wafa Hozien's professional background includes over twenty years' work as a high school history teacher and a school administrator. She has designed and delivered training for school districts, universities, and leadership academies throughout the United States and internationally. She specializes in combining research-based strategies and practical applications, working with school administrators, teacher leaders, and school districts to adopt innovative strategies for their locations. Specifically, the incorporation of issues related to culture, ethnicity, race, and religion in the education process is valued by Dr. Hozien as integral and important.

She has published numerous articles and publications on diversity issues in education. To help reduce inequities in education, Dr. Hozien makes herself available by educating through interactive workshops at schools, community organizations, and campus lectures on cultural competency and social justice. She has been researching the experiences of adolescent minority female public schooling experiences. In the multicultural education context, she has published and presented at workshops and conferences on minority student experiences.

Presently, she is an assistant professor of educational leadership at Central Michigan University, where she teaches graduate students in the principal/superintendent doctoral preparation programs. Nondiscrimination and equality are key principles that Dr. Hozien applies to education in all of her courses at Central Michigan University.

Her most recent book is *SLLA Crash Course: Approaches for Success* (Rowman & Littlefield, 2017).